THE ATHLETE'S PLAYBOOK FOR
THRIVING IN SPORT AND LIFE

mentality
wins

DR. JONATHAN HAYWOOD JENKINS and
DR. KIMBERLY H. MCMANAMA O'BRIEN

Published in Boston, Massachusetts by 65 Overtime LLC

Paperback ISBN: 979-8-218-85960-2
Ebook ISBN: 979-8-218-86884-0

Cover design by John Frits
Interior book design and typesetting by Jess LaGreca, Mayfly book design

Library of Congress Catalog Number: 2025924214
First Printing: 2026

To all of the athletes we have ever worked with—
this book is for you.

contents

PART 4: FLOURISH

introduction

Why do some athletes rise to the challenge, maintaining their composure and performing flawlessly under pressure, while others falter, overwhelmed by doubt and stress?

Why do some athletes shake off mistakes without missing a beat, while others let a single error snowball into a total meltdown?

And why do some athletes get better and better at their sport, while others plateau or even decline despite putting in the same hours of training?

The difference rarely comes from physical ability alone. Instead, it's the mental game—the ability to manage emotions, stay focused, and push through adversity—that separates good athletes from great ones.

Although we tend to associate success in sports with factors like strength, speed, and agility, the truth is that mental skills like focus, grit, and emotional self-regulation are equally important in forging champions. If two athletes are equally matched in physical skills, it's almost *always* the one with stronger mental skills who will prevail.

As sport psychology clinicians, we see this phenomenon play out all the time. Whether it's basketball, golf, gymnastics, or long-distance running, the athletes who invest in their mentality come out ahead. Stars like Michael Jordan, Serena Williams, and Jessica Long are emphatic that the mental side of their sport is way more important than the physical. They insist that once you have a baseline of physical fitness and skill, your mind is the only thing holding you back.

Yet despite these examples and countless more, many athletes still believe that reaching your full potential means doing more reps and drills, toughening up, suppressing your emotions, and sacrificing everything in the name of your sport. The athletes who come to see us are often struggling from burnout, physical injuries, and the intense emotional strain that goes along with pushing your body to the limit without enlisting your mind as an ally. We've worked with athletes who are at the very top of their sport, yet suffering so intensely that they're considering walking away.

Whether it's letting your emotions spiral out of control when you make a bad play, getting distracted in key moments, or ruthlessly criticizing yourself when you're anything less than perfect, the mental habits you bring into your sport can hold you back and rob you of the very enjoyment that brought you to that sport in the first place. But when you use the science-backed tools we teach in this book to fine-tune your mentality, you will develop the skills you need to perform your best when it matters most, and the perspective you need to enjoy yourself along the way.

WHO WE ARE

We're Jonathan and Kimberly, sport clinicians with combined decades of experience helping athletes thrive. But we're also lifelong athletes ourselves. Just like you, we know what it's like to focus too heavily on the physical side of our sport while overlooking the mental one.

Lacrosse became Jonathan's outlet after he experienced a traumatic injury in his freshman year of college—but soon, it also became his burden. He put so much pressure on lacrosse to be the "perfect" stress reliever that every mistake he made on the field felt life-threatening. Instead of walking onto the field excited to play, he just hoped he wouldn't screw up.

His therapist made what felt like a strange suggestion.

"At your next practice, I want you to drop your first pass—on purpose," he said. "That way, you can stop being so afraid of the feelings that come from making a mistake. And it will force you to practice your mental reset skills, too."

Jonathan was skeptical, but he dutifully followed his therapist's advice. At his next lacrosse practice, he intentionally dropped his first pass and felt a familiar wave of dread and embarrassment. *Man, imagine if that had been a real mistake during a real game*, he thought. *I'd never forgive myself.* With great effort, he forced himself to move through the mental reset exercise he'd worked on with his therapist: adjusting his body language to reflect ease and confidence and mentally repeating the cue phrase "flush it."

Dropping a pass felt devastating at first, but after doing it several practices in a row, Jonathan realized he was getting more and more comfortable on the field. Mistakes—even "real" ones—were no longer triggering such negative feelings. He could shake things off quickly and keep playing at a high level instead of getting sucked into a mental doom spiral that affected his performance. This experience was so eye-opening, it inspired him to become a sport psychologist.

As of this book's publication, Jonathan has spent over a decade at Massachusetts General Brigham Hospital, supporting athletes of all ages with mental health challenges and performance goals. A member of Harvard Medical School's teaching community and former assistant training director of psychology at the hospital, he is also the founder of Mental Fitness & Psychotherapy, LLC. Jonathan is currently in his ninth season as team clinical and performance psychologist for the New England Patriots, and his tenth season as behavioral sport psychologist for the Boston Red Sox.

Kim's path to sport social work also began with her experience as an athlete. She played on Harvard's national championship-winning hockey team, but secretly she was struggling. On the ice, she was constantly in her head about everything—every mistake she made, how bad she was, how embarrassed and ashamed she felt when she didn't get the playing time she wanted. Even when she became a team captain, she felt like she was constantly failing her teammates and was tormented by the fact that she could never please everybody.

When the revered sports and performance psychologist Len Zaichkowsky came to speak with her team, Kim asked to meet with him privately to work on managing her emotions and cultivating leadership skills. Those sessions changed Kim's life. If she had known then what she knows now about the importance of skills like positive self-talk and mindfulness, her experience as an athlete could have been completely different.

Kim is the founder and director of Unlimited Resilience, LLC, a group mental health practice for athletes by athletes. Since focusing her clinical social work practice on sports, Kim has worked with athletes from youth recreational all the way up to Olympic and professional levels. She conducts mental skills training with high school and college teams, does bereavement work with teams who have lost a teammate to suicide, and gives talks across the country on the topics of athlete mental health and suicide prevention.

Together, we have worked with athletes across virtually every sport and age group—from youth soccer to college rowing, Olympic figure skating to junior hockey, high school ski racing to club swimming, retired athletes to Special Olympians, scratch golfers to Paralympic medalists, and those impacted by emotional challenges and neurodevelopmental differences.

We believe mental health and athletic performance are inextricably linked. When we put in the effort to feel our best mentally, we set ourselves up to play our best. Through years of training and clinical practice, we've realized that physical talent is only one piece of the athletic puzzle; to fully thrive, you need to learn and practice the mental skills that let you take risks and play free. Cultivating a winning mentality is the secret to reaching your full potential, inside and outside of sport.

THE FOUR PILLARS OF A WINNING MENTALITY

In our decades of experience working with athletes, we've observed that truly elite performers have four things in common. First, they have the ability to **focus**. They can direct their attention where they want to, when they want to, switching smoothly between tasks and successfully filtering out distractions. This strong focus makes it easier to enter the **flow** states in which they can play freely at the height of their powers. The joy and ease arising from flow contributes to a well of positive emotion that athletes can draw on when the going gets tough, meaning they can be resilient and **finish** strong no matter what. The self-confidence this builds sets athletes up to **flourish** both in the game and in everyday life.

The four sections of this book reflect these four pillars:

FOCUS teaches you the fundamental skills of concentration and attention. You'll learn about the power of play in developing effortless focus, the role of goals and habits in directing your mental energy, and how to master the four types of attention. We'll also cover pre-performance rituals and routines and practical concentration exercises to build your ability to focus when it matters most.

FLOW centers on mindfulness as your gateway to peak performance states. You'll learn core mindfulness skills like breath awareness, body scanning, and noticing and naming thoughts and emotions. We'll talk about how to master the uncertainty inherent in sports and how to use teamwork as a springboard for flow.

FINISH focuses on building resilience and bouncing back from setbacks. You'll learn how to handle pressure instead of avoiding it, discover the power of positive self-talk, overcome perfectionism, and process mistakes without letting them define you.

FLOURISH addresses your complete well-being as an athlete and person. You'll explore your values, purpose, and identity, learn to prevent and recover from injuries and burnout, and build strong support systems—all while maintaining the perspective that you are a human first, and your sport is simply something that you do.

You can work through this book in a linear fashion or jump straight to the chapter that speaks to your most urgent need—it's up to you. Each chapter ends with a skill you can try immediately to boost your ability to focus, flow, finish, and flourish, no matter what your starting point is.

OUR PROMISE TO YOU

Our promise to you is simple but powerful: the skills in this book will give you a better chance of becoming elite in your sport while still maintaining a life you love and that truly feels like yours.

If you've ever choked under pressure, hit a plateau in your training, or felt hollow and empty—even after winning a big game or competition—this book is for you. Every athlete—from beginners to Hall of Famers—has experienced moments of doubt or even flat-out crisis. Tending to your mentality with the same care you give to your physical body will make you happier, healthier, and more effective as an athlete.

At the end of this book, you'll have a deeper understanding of yourself and the tools you need to approach your sport—and any challenge in life—with confidence and clarity. The solutions and strategies we present here are backed by sound scientific research and years of clinical practice, ensuring that every tool you learn is effective and actionable.

But as much as we want you to experience more success as an athlete, our true hope is that this book will help you discover more bliss, flow, and longevity in your sport. The real treasures of sport are the pride you feel in your effort, the friendships forged through shared struggle, and the confidence you build when you make the choice to courageously face adversity day after day. When you've already won on the inside, winning on the outside becomes less important—yet somehow easier to attain.

PART 1

focus

the power of play

Daryl was an eighteen-year-old golfer who had just been recruited to play on a Division I team when he started college the following year—but instead of feeling elated, he was filled with dread.

"I love golf," he told Jonathan in their first meeting, "I have pictures of myself as a kid, holding a driver and grinning like crazy. But somewhere along the way, it turned into a grind. I feel mentally exhausted at the end of each practice, and I've completely lost the joy."

When Jonathan asked Daryl to tell him about the last time he had fun playing golf, he grimaced. "I don't even remember, man," he said. "Maybe when I was, like, twelve?"

Jonathan had an idea. Working with Daryl's coach, they created a set of end-of-practice mini-games to help Daryl finish each training session on a fun, low-pressure note. One of these mini-games turned putting practice into a point-based challenge, with harder putts with tricky breaks worth more points. Another game revolved around targets—how many times could he hit the green from 150 yards out in ten shots? There was just one rule: no technical feedback allowed. This was pure play.

The transformation was immediate. "I started looking forward to the last thirty minutes of practice instead of gritting my teeth and getting through it," Daryl said. Soon, Daryl's teammates were joining in the mini-games, and it became a time of fun, connection, and light-hearted competition for the entire team.

The results of adding more playfulness to his training spoke for themselves. By midseason, Daryl's confidence had returned—as had his love for golf. The same sense of fun and engagement he felt during the mini-games started showing up in actual competition. By the end of the season, he'd reduced his blow-up holes by 33 percent and increased his greens in regulation by 25 percent, leading his team to several top-five and top-ten finishes—and he couldn't be more excited to keep playing.

"Those mini-games brought me back from the edge of quitting," Daryl reflected as he headed off to college. "They brought the joy back, and reminded me why I fell in love with this sport in the first place."

From Steph Curry playfully zigzagging through his pregame routine to softball players dancing in the dugout to hype up their teammates and celebrate big plays, the world of sports is filled with moments of levity and joy. Before a big game, NBA players will gather by the hoop to play "knock out" or HORSE; before a football game, teammates will compete with each other to see who can throw the football and hit the crossbar of the field goal from the furthest away. And at the end of a lacrosse practice, players often make a game of trying to hit the goal pipes, cheering when someone makes a good shot and the metal makes a satisfying clanging sound.

These seemingly trivial games and challenges serve an incredibly important purpose. They help players loosen up and release tension, temporarily distracting themselves from the pressures of the "real" training session or game. They warm up core skills when the stakes are low. They create shared experiences that bond teammates and build camaraderie. Most importantly, they remind everyone that sport should be fun and that, at the end of the day, it's all just a game.

But these athletes are just rediscovering something children have always known. If you walk past an elementary school during PE class or recess, you'll hear a chorus of happy shrieks and laughter, and see smiles on the children's faces as they race each other across the playground, shoot hoops with a basketball that looks huge in their small hands, and play a variety of games whose rules seem to change on the fly. As they play, they're developing their athletic skills: how to create a burst of speed when you're being chased, how to catch a wobbly throw, and how to notice an opponent's weak spots and take advantage of them.

It's clear that play makes us better athletes—yet the better we get, and the more serious we become about our sport, the more rarely we allow ourselves to play. As we transition from recess to recreational leagues to elite competitions, everything starts to feel like it has much higher stakes; we feel like we can't afford to "waste" time on play when we could be doing drills and getting technical feedback. We get better at our sport, but we often lose the very joy and freedom that made us fall in love with it in the first place.

When Kim tells people she played on a national championship hockey team at Harvard University, they often assume it was all work and no play. This couldn't be further from the truth! One of the biggest secrets to her team's success was that every day contained some kind of fun and games on the ice, in the locker room, and outside of the arena.

One of the team's favorite games was called Showcase Showdown. Every now and then, at the end of practice, when it seemed like the players needed something to lift their spirits, Coach Katey Stone would yell, "Showcase Showdown!"

The players would start yelling and slamming their sticks with excitement and quickly form two teams of "rooks vs. vets" to compete in a shoot-out, with the "rooks" composed of freshmen and sophomores, and "vets" of juniors and seniors. Over the course of the season, both teams came up with special handshakes, dances, and chants to pump themselves up and intimidate the competition.

The "vets" were typically louder and more boisterous going into the challenge, while the "rooks" were more strategic and discreet. Whichever team won the challenge would strut into the locker room after practice and jokingly rub in their victory as they got changed before walking to dinner. This playfulness fostered bonds of friendship that couldn't be achieved in a high-stakes environment like an actual game or a serious drill.

Thanks to games like Showcase Showdown, even the shyest athletes had the chance to come out of their shells and laugh and joke with the more outgoing ones. The playfulness also gave players a thirst to win and an ability to handle pressure that would serve them well come game time. Sometimes their desire to beat each other in Showcase Showdown was even stronger than what they felt when they played against other teams during the season!

Playing games with your team creates memories, provides the raw materials for inside jokes and other aspects of team culture, and makes big deposits into the "bank" of positive energy you can draw on in difficult moments when the stakes are much higher. When the heat is on, embodying the spirit of a playful moment in practice can help shift the team's energy and rally the players to do their best.

THE CONNECTION BETWEEN PLAY AND FOCUS

At this point, you may be wondering why we've opened the section on focus with a chapter about play. Isn't play the *opposite* of focus—just goofing around when you're supposed to be dialed in?

The truth is, play and focus aren't opposites—in fact, they're deeply intertwined. When you're doing something playful, your attention naturally becomes focused without the mental strain that goes along with forced concentration. Think about watching a child completely absorbed in building a snow fort or racing their bikes with friends. They can maintain this focused state for hours because they're genuinely enjoying themselves.

The same principle applies to athletic training. When Daryl participated in those end-of-practice mini-games, he wasn't struggling to pay attention or forcing himself to concentrate; his focus emerged organically because the games were inherently engaging. Play activates what psychologists call "effortless attention"—a state in which we're fully present and absorbed without the mental fatigue that comes from *forcing* ourselves to focus.

Many of the athletes we see in our sport psychology practices tend to mix up focus with tension or even stress. They assume that being focused means being rigid, serious, and tightly controlled—the opposite of playful. But when we're tense and overly serious, our stress increases, our decision-making suffers, and we lose the creative adaptability that sports demand. Playfulness, on the other hand, means being both alert and at ease. When you're playful, you're curious, open to possibilities, and ready to adapt on the fly—all while being deeply focused on the game you're playing.

One of the biggest enemies of athletic focus is the mental chatter that runs through our minds during training and competition—thoughts about technique, past mistakes, future outcomes, or outside pressures. Playful activities derail this overthinking by giving your mind something immediate and irresistible to focus on. When Daryl was trying to hit the green from 150 yards in ten shots, he was no longer thinking about his upcoming tournament or worrying about his coach's feedback on the last drill. Instead, he was completely absorbed in the immediate challenge of winning the game.

While drills and other standard training methods tend to rely on willpower and self-discipline to maintain focus—both of which we possess in finite supply—play develops what you might call "sustainable focus"—the ability to maintain attention over long periods without depleting your mental energy or feeling burned out. Because games and low-stakes challenges are intrinsically rewarding, you can stay focused the whole time and actually *gain* energy instead of expending it. This is why Daryl found himself looking forward to the last thirty minutes of practice and why his improved focus began showing up in actual competition. When you develop your focus through play rather than forced discipline, it becomes a renewable resource instead of a scarce commodity.

PLAY AND FLOW STATES

One of the most magical side effects of incorporating play into your athletic training is an increase in flow—that state when you're so fully engaged that time seems to stop. Play creates the perfect conditions for flow because, unlike repetitive drills that can become monotonous, playful activities are constantly presenting you with new challenges that demand your complete attention, and this helps you stay present instead of drifting off into thoughts or ruminations.

Jonathan loves running in the woods near his home in Massachusetts in part because it makes him feel like a kid. He can leap over roots, dodge muddy spots in the trail, and spontaneously sprint up hills just for the fun of it. Even though he takes his marathon training very seriously, the woods feel like an adventure playground where he can fully let go of his thoughts about work and experience the pure pleasure of running in nature—often finding himself in a flow state.

While the leaves whisper around him and flowers peek up from the forest floor, Jonathan finds himself making split-second decisions about foot placement, varying his pace to match the terrain, and occasionally taking detours to explore interesting paths—all without the rigid structure of a traditional track workout. This playful approach to running has kept his love for the sport alive, and has made him a more fluid and adaptable runner during races.

We'll discuss flow states in detail in Chapter 5. For now, the important thing to remember is that play can be a gateway to flow—not a frivolous addition to your training regimen, but a deeply valuable complement to it.

REDISCOVERING PLAY

Think of a time when you did something playful—a game of tag with a niece or nephew, getting into a snowball fight with friends, or finding yourself in an epic game of pickup basketball that lasted until dark. Chances are, you felt a sense of excitement, joy, and ease—you were probably laughing, doing some lighthearted teasing or trash-talking, and completely absorbed in the moment. Sure, you wanted to win, but winning was secondary to the sheer fun of playing. Time seemed to fly by, and even if you noticed yourself getting physically tired, you still walked away on an emotional high, already looking forward to the next time you could play.

Now ask yourself when the last time was that you felt that same sense of elation in your primary sport. Is it hard to come up with an example? If so, that's a sure sign your training routine could benefit from an injection of playfulness. If you've been highly disciplined and serious in your training for a long time, it might be hard to imagine how to make your training fun again. The key is to reach back in your memory and remember the things you loved as a kid, or simply when you were new to the game.

When you think back about your time in elementary school, you'll realize that many of the foundational skills you learned there—like reading, spelling, and counting—were taught to you through games. Maybe you learned new words with flashcards or spelling bees, or learned math by playing a version of bingo where you had to solve simple equations to discover the number being called. This element of fun helped you feel more focused and invested in the task, and helped you both learn faster and cement that learning for the long term. When a game is joyful and engaging, you want to keep playing it over and over—and keep learning more and more.

Gamifying your sports practice means applying those same techniques to your training routine. Can you incorporate things like music, obstacle courses, or mystery prizes into your training? Can you enlist your teammates in a fun challenge that gets everyone invested? Can you introduce factors like randomness or a time limit to make things surprising and unpredictable, forcing you to try new things and adapt on the fly?

The magic of gamification is that it takes your mind off "serious" goals, like winning an upcoming tournament, and directs that energy toward an immediate but less-important goal, like making it through an obstacle course. This shift reduces the performance anxiety you feel while building the exact same core skills you need for competition—a sneaky way to get you to practice the things that scare you the most.

When the stakes feel lower, your body stays relaxed and your mind stays open to learning, instead of getting locked up in the fear of failure. Gamification also breaks you out of obsessive perfectionism: instead of drilling the same technique over and over, your frustration growing, you're solving fun puzzles that *just so happen* to improve that same technique. Play encourages experimentation and creativity, helping you discover new strategies you might never have wanted to risk trying under "serious" conditions.

Here are some examples of how you can gamify different aspects of your training:

- If you play tennis, try making small tennis ball pyramids on key spots on the court and have a competition with a teammate to see who can hit the most targets in ten serves.

- If you're a runner, try playing the "alphabet game" on training runs: look for street signs or business names that start with each letter of the alphabet, working your way from A to Z.

- If you play lacrosse, try having a practice in which players receive one point for scoring with their strong hand but two points for scoring with their off hand.

- If you're a cyclist, try "landmark intervals" where you sprint between physical features of your environment like mailboxes or signs instead of using time or distance.

- If you're a boxer, write down the names of various real or imagined opponents on slips of paper and put them in a jar. Pull out one slip and practice shadowboxing that specific opponent, adapting your combinations and footwork accordingly.

Aim to gamify at least one moment in practice per week. Notice how this makes you feel. Do you feel more alert? Energized? Creative? Are you enjoying a closer connection with your teammates? Can you gamify even more elements of your training?

Don't be surprised if you start looking forward to practices or training sessions with an intensity you've never felt before—or at least, not since you were a kid.

We started this book with a chapter on play to remind you of an important truth: Developing a winning mentality as an athlete doesn't always mean doubling down on self-discipline, assigning yourself harder workouts, or implementing stricter routines. Sometimes, it means loosening up and having more fun. When you approach your sport with a spirit of playfulness, you not only enjoy it more and build stronger bonds with your teammates— you also access deeper levels of focus, creativity, and flow that elevate your performance. Games, challenges, and goofing off aren't distractions from your "real" training—they *are* real training, and they will make you great.

SKILL TO TRY: REMINDERS OF FUN

If you're the kind of athlete who tends to get overly intense and serious about your training, try surrounding yourself with reminders of fun. You can:

- Set your phone lock screen to a photo of yourself playing your sport as a kid with a huge grin on your face, enjoying your sport to its fullest.
- Keep photos of fun times with your team on your wall.
- Before a game or competition, when you're feeling a lot of stress and pressure, watch a video of yourself as a kid playing free and enjoying yourself.

Simple actions like this can increase positive emotions and remind you of your "why" when you find yourself stuck in moments of intensity or unpleasantness.

Head to www.mentalitywins.com/resources for a list of ways to gamify your practice and for journaling prompts to help you remember the fun you had playing your sport.

goals and habits

Alex was a Masters rower who had taken a couple years off following the birth of her first child. Now that her child was in daycare, she was eager to get back to winning races again. At their first meeting, Kim asked her about her goals.

"Well, first I want to get back in race shape," she said. "But my real goal is to win another Head of the Charles."

After some probing, she revealed a few obstacles that were tripping her up. "I know I need to start training on the erg again," she said. "But whenever I take my first few strokes and feel how behind I am, I feel so discouraged I just give up."

She'd also developed some unhelpful habits, like scrolling social media after training sessions to see what her former competitors were up to, making her feel even more hopeless and down on herself.

Kim immediately understood what was going wrong: Alex was so focused on her outcome goal of getting back to winning races that the training process itself felt unrewarding. Her habits needed a reset, too.

Instead of "get back in race shape," Kim suggested a process goal of simply getting on the water every day. This took away the all-or-nothing pressure that made Alex want to declare defeat. She also encouraged Alex to either delete the most anxiety-provoking social

media apps altogether or set time limits on them. Finally, she showed
her how to keep a practice journal so that she could feel a clear sense
of direction in every workout instead of just wishing she felt like she
did before having her baby.

By the time summer came around, Alex was on the water rowing
every day, and she'd started steering clear of social media, under-
standing the negative impact it had on her performance and enjoy-
ment of the sport. She decided to push back her goal of winning the
Head of the Charles by one year, giving herself more time to train. In
the meantime, she worked toward monthly fitness goals and won a
handful of smaller races.

"My original goal was actually demotivating me," she later con-
fessed to Kim. "Bringing my attention back to the process instead of
the outcome changed everything."

The French author Antoine de Saint-Exupéry once wrote "A goal
without a plan is just a wish." As athletes, we can dream all we
want about what we wish to achieve, but unless we have a plan
for doing so, it will likely never come true. Setting good goals,
developing the habits that will help you achieve them, and con-
tinuously evaluating your progress are critical to fulfilling your
dreams, as Alex found out when she attempted to pick up her
Masters rowing career where she'd left off a couple years earlier.

When you have a well-crafted goal, your mind automatically
starts looking out for things that will help you achieve it—a psychological process known as selective attention. Let's say you're
a basketball player with a goal of getting your feet set before every
shot. Before you know it, you'll be noticing all kinds of things
about your foot positioning throughout practice—including

things you'd never noticed before. A good goal directs your focus, and this makes your training way more efficient.

Without clear goals, you might waste your practice time on skills you've already mastered, neglecting the things you really need to work on. A goal gives you the focus you need to prioritize tasks during precious training hours. When you know what your goal is, you hit the ground running, your mind and body already primed to learn and improve. If your performance is inconsistent, you've hit a plateau, you feel unfocused during practice, or you're drowning in a state of plain old overload, setting the right types of goals can be the silver bullet you need to get yourself back on track.

PROCESS GOALS AND OUTCOME GOALS

There are two main types of goals you'll encounter as an athlete: outcome-oriented and process-oriented goals. **Outcome goals** focus on a concrete, measurable endpoint: for example, a swimmer aiming to drop five seconds off their 200-meter freestyle time, or a basketball player wanting to improve their free throw percentage from 70 percent to 85 percent by the end of the season.

In contrast, **process goals** are about doing the behaviors that improve the likelihood that you'll reach your outcome goals. For example, if you're a lacrosse goalie with an outcome goal of having the highest save percentage in the league, a process goal would be to make a good play on every shot. If you're a triathlete who gets exhausted during a swim, you can set the process goal of breathing every three strokes instead of every five. If you're a tennis player who tends to get fixated on the score, you can set the process goal of mentally resetting yourself during changeovers to help you stay composed in the moment.

Although it's good to have a mix of outcome and process goals, you want to be careful not to fixate too much on outcome goals. This is because outcome goals tend to involve many aspects that are simply beyond your control. Let's say you're a lacrosse goalie. There are many factors related to your save percentage that are out of your control, such as your competitors' shot speed and accuracy, the shooter's proximity to the cage, the unpredictability of bounce shots, etc. If you get fixated on having the highest save percentage above all else, you might beat yourself up for things that were outside your control, and this will unnecessarily deteriorate your confidence.

In contrast, a process goal keeps you focused on what you *can* control, like making a good play on every shot. As a goalie in lacrosse, you can be in the best possible position, use perfect technique, be mentally locked in, and still get scored on. If you achieve your process goal and get scored on anyway, you'll feel a lot less defeated and a lot prouder of yourself than if you were focused on a specific outcome.

Here are some examples of outcome goals and process goals for various sports, along with strategies for achieving them:

Sport	Outcome Goal	Process Goal	Plan/ Strategies
Hockey	Score fifty goals this season	Improve shot speed, accuracy, quick release	Shoot one hundred pucks a day, with targets
Golf	Break ninety	Improve consistency off the tee, putting stroke, bunker saves	Take thirty greenside bunker shots a day and try to reduce 3-putts from wherever it lands
Rowing	Get erg 2K under 7:25	Improve mobility, back strength, cardiovascular endurance	Practice erg 2K biweekly and aim to meet splits consistently
Baseball	Bat .300 for the season	Improve ability to see pitches, take bad pitches, and better understand hitting heat zones	One hundred purposeful swings in the batting cage with at least 50 percent of pitches being ones that are the most challenging

Setting good goals means hitting the right balance between being ambitious and being kind to yourself. Your outcome goals should require real effort to achieve—but they shouldn't be so impossible that you run your body into the ground or fall into despair. A good outcome goal should give you a slightly nervous, tingly feeling when you think about it, not a wave of dread. Similarly, good process goals should be doable even when you're tired, stressed, or having a bad day. You should be able to say, "I did well—I remembered to breathe," even when nothing else goes your way.

SMART GOALS AND UNSTRUCTURED GOALS

Modern sport psychology and psychology in general have been hyperfocused on goal setting that is SMART (Specific, Measurable, Achievable, Relevant, and Time-Specific). SMART goals became popular after researchers found that vague goals like "try harder" or "be a better teammate" were dismally ineffective at helping athletes improve. Humans need concrete targets to work toward—otherwise, we have no way of measuring our progress and no rush of satisfaction when we get closer to our goal. SMART goals aim to solve this problem by making goals crystal clear, achievable, and time-limited.

Here's an example of a SMART goal for a long-distance runner:

Specific: Complete a marathon.
Measurable: Finish in under four hours.
Achievable: Follow a training plan that includes running four times a week.

Relevant: Aligns with the goal of increasing mental fortitude and physical stamina.

Time-bound: The race is one year away.

As you can see, this SMART goal leaves little room for ambiguity. There's a clear metric for success and a clear timeline—the goal doesn't get lost in a vague "sometime" that might never come. If you're that long-distance runner, you'll feel a sense of urgency as that one-year deadline approaches, motivating you to stick to your training routine.

Yet for all their benefits, SMART goals aren't right for every athlete, every time—and they aren't the *only* kind of goal that's worthwhile to pursue. For some athletes, SMART goals can feel overly restrictive. They don't give you much freedom to course-correct when unexpected challenges arise. Remember that marathon you planned to run in under four hours? What happens when you sprain your ankle and have to stop running for six weeks? If you stick too rigidly to your SMART goal, you might rush back into training too quickly, at the risk of worsening your injury—or you might abandon your goal entirely and lose motivation. The very same specificity that made your goal so effective has now become a liability.

SMART goals can also backfire when you're doing something you're very new at or have never tried before. For example, let's say you're learning to bowl for the first time. As a beginner, you have no way of knowing which approach will help you learn the fastest. If you set a SMART goal, you might become discouraged—and you might find yourself barking up the wrong tree, working on a skill that isn't appropriate for you at that moment in your learning. Situations like this call for an unstructured approach to optimize learning while nurturing your emotional health.

The counterpart to SMART goals is unstructured goals. An unstructured goal is like a SMART goal's rascally younger sibling. Whereas a SMART goal emphasizes metrics and timeline, an unstructured goal is all about exploration, learning, and making discoveries.

The first type of unstructured goal that you most likely experienced as a child at school or summer camp was a do-your-best or "open" goal—also known as "just go out and have fun." Open goals deemphasize maximum achievement. Instead, they encourage you to explore your potential talent in a given skill or sport. When you engage in a do-your-best goal, you're open and curious. You might make mistakes, fumble, or feel completely out of your element, but it doesn't matter because the point is to have a new experience, not demonstrate your mastery.

Even if you're an elite athlete, you probably encounter do-your-best goals a lot more often than you realize. If you've ever gone to a hot yoga class, accepted a buddy's invitation to try rock climbing or backcountry skiing, or tried surfing while on vacation, chances are you didn't go in with a rigid metric for success—instead, you just went out there to have fun and find out what you were capable of.

The benefits of open goals go way beyond the activity itself. When you're monkeying around on gymnastics equipment for the first time or trying out your friend's new e-foil, you're exposing yourself to new types of movement that can enhance your primary sport in surprising ways. In the midst of the novelty, you forget about being perfect and take pride in your attempts and in small wins instead of expecting instant mastery. You may even experience "beginner's mind" as you become absorbed in the new activity, dropping old ideas about who you are and what you can and cannot do.

Of course, some athletes who have a strong drive for mastery may find open goals vague and unsatisfying, as they lack a clear enough metric for success and don't offer the same opportunities to hone specific skills. If this is you, open goals can work best as occasional supplements to your primary training. Try using them during recovery periods or as a way to try completely new activities. The key is realizing that different types of goals serve different purposes—they're not one-size-fits-all.

EVALUATING GOALS

Setting meaningful goals is just the beginning. The real payoff comes when you evaluate your goals on a regular basis, ideally with the help of a coach, teammate, or sport clinician.

Kim's most important individual goal while playing hockey at Harvard was to get a regular shift. She knew that her skill didn't compare to the majority of her teammates, but her passion and work ethic were unmatched.

In her Junior season, Kim's coach told her that if she wanted more time on the ice, she needed to skate faster and make better decisions with the puck. To improve her speed, Kim made a point of doing extra ice sprints at the end of every single practice, as well as extra bike sprints three times a week. To improve her decision-making, Kim studied the systems and worked on managing her performance anxiety so she wouldn't throw away the puck when she should have held onto it longer. She reflected on her progress on the walk back to dinner after each practice and checked in with her coach as needed to make sure she was still on track. By the end of the season, Kim earned a regular shift in the first two periods of the National Championship game.

To effectively set and evaluate your goals, try scheduling a preseason, midseason, and postseason meeting with your coach focused on goal-setting and assessment of progress (if you don't have a coach, team up with a fellow athlete, a friend, or counselor). In the preseason meeting, you and your coach can discuss your expectations for the season and for your specific contribution to the team. Together, you can come up with a short list of shared goals, including both outcome and process goals. At midseason, you can evaluate your progress on these goals and make new ones if desired. Your postseason meeting offers an opportunity to reflect on the season as a whole and decide on offseason goals.

Goals lose their meaning if you don't evaluate and adjust them on a regular basis. And when that happens, you can find yourself going through the motions without any real purpose or passion. For example, let's say you set a goal to run a 5k in less than twenty-five minutes, and you achieve this goal early in the season. If you don't reevaluate your goal, you might end up coasting for the rest of the season without further challenges to motivate you. Similarly, if you set an overly ambitious goal of running a 5k in less than fifteen minutes but fail to re-evaluate when your mind and body hit a wall, you might phone it in for the rest of the season, having quietly decided your goal is impossible.

At least once a month, ask yourself: Are my goals still relevant to where I want to go? Am I making progress, or have I stalled? Have circumstances changed in such a way that I need to adapt my goal in some way? Changing your goal doesn't make you a failure—it means you have the wisdom to fine-tune things when you're experiencing injury, burnout, or disengagement. The important thing is maintaining your core commitment to improvement.

KEEP A TRAINING JOURNAL

A training journal is a powerful tool for tracking and evaluating your goals. It can help to keep a list of your season goals at the top of each page. Beneath your season goals, you can list a goal or two for each specific day of training. For example, if you're a golfer and your goal for the season is to break seventy-five, your goal for one training session may be to sink your putt in two or less once on the green.

Writing down a specific goal for each practice session helps you focus on the particular aspect of your game you most want to work on. Being intentional about meeting your goals prevents you from tuning out and going through the motions at practice. At the end of your training session, revisit your journal and do a quick reflection on how well you did with respect to your goals for the day. Make a note of what didn't go so well, but also write down any small wins for the day. This will allow you to pay attention to the positives, boost confidence, and keep forward momentum.

Here's an example of a daily training journal for a golfer:

Season Goal:	Break Seventy-Five
Today's goal/intention:	Sink putt in two or less once on green
Strategies to use:	Deep breath before each putt Make sure I am lined up correctly Mind clear and focused and positive before putt Focus on stroke
Reflections:	Was intentional about breathing, which helped me relax and stay calm and consistent and not rush it Stroke speed was off at times, need to focus on that next time

When evaluating progress toward your goals, try to remember that it is rare to see huge results in short periods of time. Kim's strength and conditioning coach, Jonas Weichmann, frequently reminds his athletes of the importance of "getting one percent better every day." By making a commitment to your training regimen and holding yourself accountable to those habits and routines day after day, the results will come naturally in time.

BUILDING GOOD HABITS

Strong habits are the key to achieving your goals as an athlete because they establish consistency in both your physical training and mental preparation. You can either develop healthy habits that reinforce a sense of calm and confidence, or you can slip into habits that tear down your self-esteem and create mental weakness.

Although we tend to think of habits as something we actively create, the truth is we're constantly forming habits whether we're consciously aware of it or not. Every action you take, from the moment you wake up in the morning to the moment you go to sleep at night, reinforces some kind of habit. Do you brush your teeth? Scroll on your phone on the bus or subway? Scarf down an energy bar between classes? Although you may not have invested much mental energy into forging these habits, they became habitual simply through repetition.

In his book *Atomic Habits*, the author and former college baseball player James Clear outlines four strategies for creating a good habit and making it stick: 1) make it obvious, 2) make it attractive, 3) make it easy, and 4) make it satisfying.

Let's say you're a soccer player who's feeling unmotivated to do your running conditioning but knows you need to establish a running habit to be ready for preseason. You can make it obvious by scheduling a two-mile run in your calendar each day and setting an alert to remind you. You can make it attractive by planning to stop at a nearby convenience store to get an ice-cold G Fit right after your run. You can make it easy by putting your running gear out on your desk the night before. And you can make it satisfying by putting a check mark in your training journal after each run, showing that you accomplished what you set out to do.

Elite athletes don't rely on motivation—they rely on habit. As Mets All-Star Francisco Lindor said in a 2025 interview, "I'm not motivated, I'm disciplined. Motivation comes and goes." Motivation is unreliable. It fluctuates from day to day and hour to hour. If you depend on motivation to achieve your goals, you will undoubtedly be inconsistent. Instead, commit to forming strong habits.

One of the best gifts you can give yourself as an athlete is to design your environment for success. This means stripping away any obstacles that stand between you and your goal while *creating* obstacles to habits that don't serve you. For example, if the pile of dirty dishes on the counter always stops you from getting out the door to run in the morning, wash them every night before you go to bed (or at least pile them in a place where you won't see them!). If your video game console is easily accessible and distracting you from training, try keeping it at a friend's house, thereby increasing the "friction" you need to overcome in order to use it. The point is to build supportive systems into your day so that you never have to rely on willpower to execute a task. Strong routines will beat out motivation every time.

Habits can also provide sanctuary when you're stressed or when you find yourself in a tough situation. When you're dealing with the devastation of an injury or navigating an interpersonal conflict with a coach or teammate, habits can give you a sense of calm, predictability, and stability in the midst of the storm. By investing in good habits during times of low stress, you'll have something to lean on when the pressure's high, and you won't be scrambling for something to hold on to.

WHAT TO DO WHEN YOU DRIFT

Inevitably, situations will arise that throw you off your habits—things like illnesses, travel, or new demands on your time and attention. Instead of beating yourself up for falling off the wagon, take the time to explore what threw you off and brainstorm safeguards you can use when similar situations come up in the future. For example, let's say your habit of going for a run at 11 a.m. every day was thrown off when your cousins came to visit from out of town, and you felt the need to drop everything to entertain them for a week. You could establish safeguards by:

- Letting future visitors know that you go for a run every day at 11 a.m., and planning activities for them to do during that time.
- Moving your run to the early morning, before your visitors wake up.
- Scheduling a shorter run at 11 a.m. each day so you preserve the habit even if you spend less time doing it during that particular week.

Safeguards help you preserve your hard-won habit, and protect you from the frustration and disappointment that can arise when you slip on a habit that took a lot of effort to establish. They act as a buffer between you and the all-or-nothing thinking that can derail even the healthiest of habits, reminding you that an imperfectly applied habit is still better than nothing. By having these protective measures in place, you preempt potential breaking points, ensuring that one missed day doesn't unravel weeks or months of dedicated effort.

Goals and habits go hand in hand. Your goals give you direction, while your habits give you traction. In the words of football player and coach Paul "Bear" Bryant, "It's not the will to win that matters—everyone has that. It's the will to prepare to win that matters." When you pay close attention to the goals you're setting and the habits you're forming, you're preparing your mind to win, a process that is every bit as important as preparing your body to perform.

SKILL TO TRY: STOP/START/CONTINUE

This is a simple exercise, first developed by psychologist Phil Daniels, that generates three lists to come up with a strategic plan to meet your goals.

First, make a list of unhelpful habits or behaviors you'd like to **stop**.

Next, make a list of new habits and strategies you'd like to **start**.

Finally, make a list of helpful things you are already doing—habits you want to **continue**.

Here is an example of a Stop/Start/Continue exercise for a college hockey player:

Stop	Start	Continue
• Hitting snooze so that I don't miss breakfast before lift	• Visualizing scoring goals at night and before games	• Getting to practice thirty minutes early to shoot pucks
• Getting down on myself if I do not get a point in a game	• Replacing negative self-talk with positive self-talk	• Being in bed by 10:30

Head to www.mentalitywins.com/resources for a downloadable Start/Stop/Continue worksheet you can use for your own goal-setting.

pregame rituals and routines

Brittany was a thirty-year-old former collegiate runner preparing for her first Boston Marathon. Even though she was excited about finally running in her hometown race, she started to feel anxious as the race inched closer. Before practice runs, her mind would race, her heart would beat faster, and she'd feel like she couldn't breathe fully. Her performance began to suffer as she struggled to hit her usual times during tempo and even Zone 2 steady-state runs.

In her first meeting with Jonathan—who has run the Boston Marathon twice—she told him she didn't want to "let her friends and the run club down," since she knew they would be watching and cheering her on. Jonathan reassured her this concern was completely normal and that her body and mind were having typical reactions to stress.

To address Brittany's anxiety, Jonathan proposed a prerace routine to help her ground herself physically and emotionally, setting herself up to start the race in a less agitated state. Brittany's prerace routine included a breathing and visualization exercise, a cue word to help bring her back to her intention of being loose and relaxed, a written mantra on her wrist to remind her of her strength, and a mindfulness script to practice immediately before a run to position her mind in a more comfortable place.

Brittany incorporated these routines into her practices and preparation, and she slowly began feeling and performing like herself again. Although the anxiety was still present at times, Brittany felt better equipped to cope with it and prevent it from reaching such a high intensity. With practice, Brittany's prerace routine became as crucial to her runs as her running shoes and Spotify playlist.

A week after the marathon, Brittany met with Jonathan to review her experience. Like most marathons, hers didn't go as planned—she cramped early on during an unexpectedly rainy and cold day—but she finished strong and was ecstatic about her experience.

"Having that routine in place set me up to do my best," she said. "I'll never run without it!"

Whether you're a beginner or an elite athlete, you probably have something in common with the best players in your sport: a pre-game ritual or routine.

A pre-competition **routine** has a direct relationship to the physical task you're about to perform—for example, shadow-boxing in the locker room before heading into the ring, visualizing a ski race, or going through a stretching and mindfulness routine before running a marathon. A pre-competition **ritual** is a symbolic gesture that puts you in the right mental and emotional space to perform your best—for example, kneeling in prayer or listening to a certain album before you go onto the basketball court.

Let's take a closer look at rituals and routines and see how each one can help you perform your best.

RITUALS

Engaging in a **ritual** before you compete not only calms your mind but also aligns you with your higher purpose. For example, if you kiss a picture of your family before you compete, you're using your love for them—and the reminder of their love for you—as a source of strength and solace. This action not only helps you stay emotionally resilient during competition but also provides extra incentive for you to give it your all because you want to honor your family through your performance.

Rituals like these are helpful because they remind you that you're more than just an athlete—you're a fully-fledged human being, and other facets of your life will benefit when you give your absolute all in this moment. Rituals connect you to your "why": your bigger purpose for pushing yourself, whether that's your family and friends, a cause you hold dear, or a value you cherish. They can also have a calming effect, deflecting unhelpful nerves and anxiety by narrowing your focus.

Even though pregame rituals may look a lot like superstition, there's an important distinction. A superstition is the belief that a specific behavior, no matter how silly or random, will bring good luck to yourself or your team. A ritual, on the other hand, isn't random or inappropriate—it emerges from your unique personality, values, and purpose, both in your life as an athlete and beyond.

LeBron James's famous chalk toss is the perfect example of how a ritual can center on a cherished value—in this case, appreciation for fans. What started as a practical need—using powder to improve his grip on the ball—evolved into a meaningful ritual when James noticed how excited fans became watching him do it. He turned it into a theatrical moment, tossing the powder high into the air before each game to acknowledge and energize the crowd.

New Zealand's rugby team, the All Blacks, perform the Haka before each game—a traditional Māori war dance that honors values of identity, respect, and unity. By incorporating the Haka into modern sport, the All Blacks remind themselves and their fans that they represent something much larger than just a rugby team. This striking ritual also creates an intense bond between teammates as they chant and move in unison.

If you'd like to incorporate ritual into your preparation for competition, ask yourself what you value most deeply. Is it family? Community? An aspect of your identity or cultural heritage? A quality like playfulness or kindness?

You can also ask yourself questions like, *What's my favorite memory of playing this sport?* And, *What do I hope to accomplish in the future in this sport?* Engaging in this type of deep self-examination will help you identify what matters most to you and what motivates you to not only play the sport but also play it at a high level.

When you take the time to explore these questions, you'll identify the people, places, and things that give your life meaning. You'll know what and to whom you wish to dedicate your effort when playing sports and competing.

ROUTINES

In contrast to a ritual, a pre-competition **routine** primes your mind by engaging you in a light introduction to the upcoming activity. Think of it like entering the shallow end of the pool before swimming in the deep end.

Michael Phelps, the world's most decorated male swimmer, has a detailed pre-competition routine he uses consistently before every race. He begins ninety minutes before the race with a specific warm-up routine, including stretching, stroke styles and drills, and sprints to raise his heart rate. At forty-five minutes before race time, he puts on his suit; at thirty minutes, he completes his warm-up; at ten minutes, he finds a quiet place to sit with his goggles, towel, and earbuds to visualize the race and how he wants to perform. Finally, at race time, he steps onto the starting block in the same way every time. This consistency gives him a heightened sense of control and confidence.

But preparation doesn't have to be quite so time-consuming and elaborate. Nat Coutu, a lacrosse player at Stonehill College, does fifteen minutes of meditation and visualization while sitting on the Normatec, then dances with her teammates in the locker room. "At the end of the day," she says, "it's a privilege to play a college sport, and you only get so many game days!" Her approach emphasizes both focus and joy.

Meanwhile, Cam McCarthy, from Loyola University Maryland, prefers meditation and gentle instrumental music over revving himself up with loud, upbeat fight songs before a lacrosse game. "I feel I am able to concentrate far better and just remain calm," he explains.

Pre-competition routines help you transition fully to the task that awaits you, no matter what else you've been doing with your day. For instance, if you're a college student, you probably spend most of your day in a classroom, with your mind focused on taking notes and asking questions. When it comes time for sports practice, a pre-competition routine lets you transition gracefully out of "student mode" and into "athlete mode." This means you're "locked-in" and ready to go as soon as practice begins, instead of having to gradually warm up during practice and only reaching the optimal mindset when the session is half-way over.

Unlike rituals, which can be performed the same way no matter which sport you're playing, pregame routines are custom-tailored to the task at hand. For example, if you're a skier, your pre-competition routine for a slalom is going to look different than your routine for a downhill race. The stretches, visualizations, and other tasks you complete as part of your routine are closely paired to the event in question. This means that multisport athletes need to develop multiple pregame routines, which can be a time-consuming process. A coach or sport clinician can help you fine-tune your routine for every different event, making sure you're optimally prepared for each one.

PUTTING IT ALL TOGETHER

If you'd like to perform your best, incorporate both ritual *and* routine before your games and competitions. While ritual will help you connect to your higher purpose and remind you of the sources of love and support in your life, routine will prepare your mind for the physical tasks ahead and help you shift your focus to the present moment.

Try observing your teammates, as well as any professional athletes you admire. Which rituals and routines do they use, and why? Can you use any of those elements in your own practice?

You can also use this list to get you started:

- **Mindfulness:** Come into the present moment by meditating, observing your surroundings, or paying attention to physical sensations.

- **Breathing exercises:** Take slow, deep breaths, or count your inhales and exhales to activate your body's relaxation response.

- **Visualization:** Mentally rehearse your performance by imagining how you'd like to move and react during a competition.

- **A warm-up/stretching routine:** Go through a preparation sequence that activates your muscles and gets your body ready for the specific demands of your sport.

- **Reciting mantras:** Choose words or phrases that reflect your goals, values, or the mindset you'd like to cultivate, such as "trust the process" or "calm and present."

- **Talking to certain teammates:** Identify teammates who help you feel calm, confident, or energized, and make a point to connect with them before each competition.

- **Listening to specific music:** Choose songs that either pump you up or calm your nerves, depending on what your mind and body need most.

- **Wearing a specific piece of clothing or jewelry:** Pick items that have personal meaning, like a gift from a relative or something representing an important memory or experience that will remind you of your purpose and values.

When Kim played on Harvard's hockey team, she would stretch and listen to a mixtape on her Walkman (yes, she knows she's old!) in the same section of the rink with the exact same songs every time. After she got dressed, she'd always tape up her teammate's elbow pads while the team listened to the same pregame pump-up mix in the locker room. This ritual made her feel useful and helped regulate her nervous system while steadily transitioning her focus to the demands of the game.

Each time Jonathan starts a workout, he blows three kisses to the sky: one for himself, one for his son, and one for his partner. This ritual brings him a sense of peace and reminds him of why the workout is important: so he can stay healthy and spend more time with them. He treats his workouts as acts of love for his family—something that not only brings joy to his heart but also reinforces his commitment to them.

Our pregame rituals and routines have become core to who we are as athletes, connecting us to our values and preparing us to compete as our highest selves, both mentally and physically.

As you develop your own unique pregame rituals and routines, remember there's no one-size-fits-all solution. The key is to find rituals and routines that align with your personality, values, and sport-specific needs. Over time, these practices will become as essential to your performance as any piece of equipment—a reliable way to show up as your best self when you need it most.

SKILL TO TRY: TEST AND REFINE YOUR ROUTINE

Over the next week, experiment with adding one new element to your pregame preparation—whether it's a ritual that connects you to your values or a routine that helps you focus. Notice how this new element affects your mood and performance. Did it help you feel more centered? More focused? Happier?

Experiment with new elements on a regular basis until you land on a combination that's just so good you don't want to change it anymore.

Head to www.mentalitywins.com/resources for a downloadable worksheet to help you plan and evaluate your pregame routine and ritual.

training your attention

Kathleen was a college hockey goalie who knew her job was simple in theory: track the puck, stay focused, and make the save. But as games went on, she'd get so nervous her mind would scatter in a million directions. She'd start anticipating all the things that might happen instead of paying attention to what was actually going on. Before she knew it, the puck would slip past her peripheral vision, and she'd realize she'd been totally absent right when she needed her focus to be sharpest.

In her first session with Kim, Kathleen was visibly distressed. "I feel like my brain is betraying me," she said, on the edge of tears. "I tell myself to focus on the puck, but it's like I have a mental block and can't do it."

Kim knew this was a classic focus problem. She took out a hockey puck and placed it on her desk.

"Pick a spot on this logo with the shield on it," Kim said. "Just one tiny spot. Now focus everything you have on that spot. When you catch your mind wandering, say the word 'shield' and bring your attention back to that spot."

For three minutes, Kathleen stared at a tiny section of the puck's logo. Every few seconds, she'd say "shield" and refocus her attention.

It felt silly at first, but Kim explained that by practicing focus when she was off the ice, she'd have a better chance of summoning it during a game.

Kathleen started doing this focus practice at home every day. Soon, she was doing it on the ice as well. She significantly improved her ability to refocus on the puck and mentally reengage with the game. Before long, she had stopped giving up soft goals and had regained her confidence in her ability.

In the 2025 NCAA women's basketball tournament, Sarah Ashlee Barker of the University of Alabama women's basketball team put on an absolute masterclass in focus and concentration in the face of pressure. She was fouled on a game-tying three-point attempt and made all three free throws with 0.7 seconds left in regulation, forcing double overtime against Maryland.

When a big moment in a game makes emotions run high, a seemingly simple task like a free throw becomes way harder to execute. You might experience sensory overload as fans shout and chant, notice the bright lights beaming down on you, or feel cameras snapping your picture from the sidelines. Meanwhile, your inner world might be going haywire—your heart rate spiking, muscles tensing, and your mind flooding with thoughts like "Don't miss" or "Oh crap, everyone's watching."

In this kind of pressure-cooker moment, champions like Barker set themselves apart from the pack not by avoiding the internal and external overload, but by finding calm within it. They've trained their minds to cut through the noise—to hear their own breathing over the roaring crowd, feel their feet planted firmly on the ground, and trust in the skills they've practiced instead of caving into the instinct to do something panicked or rushed. For athletes like Barker, a focused mind has become the norm, not the exception.

At this point, you might be wondering why we didn't start the Focus section of the book with this chapter. Why not jump straight into attention training? The answer is simple: the kind of focus Barker showed in that basketball tournament doesn't exist in a vacuum. If you're burned out from a training regimen that's all work and no play, you'll struggle to concentrate, no matter how many focus drills you practice. If you're drifting without clear goals, you might end up applying your focus to things that aren't very important or that you've already mastered. And if you don't have a solid pregame routine, it will be much harder for you to come into a focused state, no matter how much you train your attention.

The elements we've covered so far—play, goals, rituals, and routines—create the optimal conditions for focus to flourish. They boost your happiness, lower your stress, and reduce the mental clutter that can interfere with concentration. Now that you have that foundation in place, we can build the specific skills that will allow you to summon focus in the moments you need it most.

THE FOUR TYPES OF FOCUS

Robert Nideffer is a pioneering sport psychologist whose research revealed that elite athletes don't just concentrate harder—they use their attention in different ways. He identified four distinct types of attention that athletes must use to play their best. Understanding these types of attention and knowing when and how to switch between each one is the secret to unlocking your full potential in sports.

Broad external focus means taking in the big picture of what's happening around you. Let's say you're a wheelchair basketball point guard scanning the court to see what all the other players are doing, or a soccer midfielder reading the entire field to spot an opening for a pass. Both of these moments require broad external focus—the ability to perceive the larger patterns at play instead of getting hung up on insignificant details.

Narrow external focus means tuning out everything except for one crucial detail. Some examples of this would be a golfer focusing on a spot behind the ball, or a batter tracking the pitcher's release point. When you deploy narrow external focus, you shut out everything else and give your full attention to that one tiny thing.

So far, we've covered two forms of focus that center on what's happening *outside* of you—the terrain, other players, and any equipment you might be using. But you also need to be able to focus on what's happening *inside* of you.

Broad internal focus means keeping a bird's-eye view of your mental state, emotions, and physical sensations. If you're running a marathon, you'd use broad internal focus to keep track of your energy levels and emotional state, so you can adjust your pace or tap into a source of encouragement and strength.

Narrow internal focus means concentrating on one specific aspect of your inner experience, whether it's mental, physical, or emotional. For example, if you're lifting weights, you might place a narrow focus on the feeling of driving through your heels; if you're about to do a free throw, you might focus on a mantra or cue word.

To be truly great at your sport, you need to hone your ability to shift between these four types of attention in response to the ever-changing demands of your game or competition. Having strong focus isn't enough—you also need *flexible* focus, and that means knowing when to zoom out for the big picture and when to zoom in on crucial details, when to look outward at the game, and when to turn inward to your body and mind.

TRAINING YOUR FOCUS

Chances are, some of these four types of focus come more easily to you than others. Maybe you're a natural at scanning the field and reading the play, but you struggle with smaller details. Or it's easy for you to tune out a roaring crowd during a free throw, but you can forget to eat for an entire day because you don't pay attention to your physical state overall.

The good news is, building your ability to focus is just like building strength in the gym. Although it's true that we all possess some innate abilities, with the right training program you can increase your skills in all four areas significantly. Here are some ways you can strengthen each one.

BROAD EXTERNAL FOCUS

Peripheral Vision Practice: The next time you're at a busy gym, airport, or shopping mall, find a place where you can sit still for a few minutes. Gazing straight ahead without moving your head, start making a mental list of everything you can see. This will train you to take in information from your entire visual field, whether or not you're looking directly at something.

Bird's-Eye View: The next time you're watching your sport on TV or streaming it over the internet, try narrating everything you see happening on the screen out loud—not just the main action, but details like player positioning, spacing, and patterns of movement. What do you notice yourself noticing?

NARROW EXTERNAL FOCUS

Tracking Practice: The next time you watch your sport, choose one detail, such as a certain player's left shoe, and try to track it throughout the entire game, no matter how many exciting distractions are going on. Notice what pulls your attention away from your object of focus—are you distracted by thoughts? Boredom? More "important" details of the game?

I Spy: The next time you're watching a game from the bench or stands, enlist a friend or teammate to play "I Spy" with you. Have them choose small details of the environment for you to "spy" amidst the chaos. This game does not only have to be strictly visual. For example, you can also play "I Spy" with sounds by seeking out specific noises or voices in your environment. The goal is to use your senses to notice small details and be able to pick them out of the chaos.

BROAD INTERNAL FOCUS

Body Scan: While you're doing light exercise like jogging or stretching, practice checking in with different parts of your body. How do your feet feel? Your breathing? Your energy level? Your mood? If you were a character in a video game, how many "hearts" or health points would you have?

Weather Report: Practice giving yourself quick "internal weather reports" during breaks in practice. For example, you might mentally say the words, "Physically feeling strong with good energy. Mentally sharp but sort of ruminating over nailing the next drill. Emotional state is eight out of ten but trending higher." You can also do this practice out loud with a friend or teammate to keep it engaging.

NARROW INTERNAL FOCUS

Single-Point Breathing: Find a quiet place to sit and set a timer for five minutes. During that time, focus exclusively on the sensation of air entering and leaving your nostrils. Whenever your mind wanders, gently return your attention to that one sensation.

One Muscle at a Time: The next time you're stretching, try focusing exclusively on the sensation in one specific muscle group. For example, while you're stretching your hamstrings, only pay attention to those muscles—do your best to ignore the feeling in your hips, shoulders, etc.

RECOGNIZE, RESET, RESPOND

As you work with these four methods of attention, one obstacle will always come up: mind-wandering. Whether you're scanning the playing field for a big-picture view of the game or zeroing in on your golf swing, distraction will always be waiting in the wings, finding ways to lure your mind away. It's unrealistic to *never* have your mind wander—the important thing is to have a reliable system for getting back on track with minimal downtime.

Kim's colleague Emily Lorry, CMPC, has a sport psychology technique she learned and now uses for building focus called the Three R's: Recognize, Reset, and Respond. Here's how it works:

Step 1: Recognize. The first step is simply noticing that your mind has wandered. This might sound obvious, but it's often the hardest part. Many athletes spend entire possessions or even games mentally checked out without realizing it. Are you thinking about the last mistake you made? Worried about what might happen next? Distracted by crowd noise or an opponent's trash talk? The moment you catch yourself thinking about anything other than the immediate task at hand, you've successfully completed step one.

Step 2: Reset. Once you've recognized that your focus has drifted, it's time to hit the mental reset button. This could be as simple as taking one deep breath, saying a cue word or phrase like "focus" or "lock back in," or doing a quick body check to release tension. When Jonathan was playing collegiate lacrosse, his reset cue phrase was "flush it" because it made him think of flushing a crappy play down the toilet and moving on. Not only did this cue phrase snap him back into the present moment, but it also made him laugh and lifted him out of his funk after a bad play.

Step 3: Respond. The final step is immediately redirecting your attention to the most important thing happening in the present moment. For a basketball player, this might mean finding the ball and identifying where teammates and opponents are positioned. For a tennis player, it could mean focusing on the opponent's serve toss. For a soccer goalkeeper, it's tracking the ball and reading the developing play. The key is having a predetermined target for your attention so you're not just hoping your focus will return on its own.

Early on, you might find yourself cycling through all three steps over and over again during the course of a single game or practice session. You'll notice your mind has drifted, reset with your cue word, and respond by refocusing on the game—only to catch your thoughts wandering again just moments later. If this is you, don't worry—this is *completely* normal. It doesn't mean the technique isn't working; it means you're slowly building the mental muscle you need to sustain your focus for longer and longer periods.

Remember, the goal isn't to become a Zen master who never has a wandering thought—it's to notice these lapses faster and respond more effectively. With consistent practice, the recognize-reset-respond process becomes so automatic that you can refocus almost instantly, turning moments of distraction into brief blips instead of zoning out for long chunks of your training or playing. Eventually, you'll find that simply recognizing your mind has wandered is enough to snap your attention back to where it needs to be, cutting out the reset and respond steps entirely.

The ability to direct your focus is one of the most powerful tools you can develop as an athlete. Unlike physical skills that can plateau or decline with age, you can keep on honing your focusing skills throughout your athletic career and beyond. Even though other players may be bigger, stronger, or faster than you, you can still be the best at focusing—and that's no small advantage. Whether you're using the Three R's to refocus during a crucial moment or strengthening your peripheral vision during the off-season, you're developing your ability to perceive the world clearly, both inside and outside of you.

SKILL TO TRY: OBJECT STARE

Try this three-part mental drill to increase your ability to focus.

First, find an object from your sport, like a ball, stick, or uniform, and place it directly in front of you.

For the first step, focus your attention on a specific spot on the object. As you keep your eyes on that specific spot, slowly repeat to yourself a word or phrase related to the object such as "tape," "red," or "ball." Every time you catch your attention drifting, repeat this concentration cue to help yourself focus again.

Practice this for one to two minutes.

For the second part, close your eyes and try to call up a visual image of the object and the specific spot on the object you chose. Continue to repeat your concentration cue every time your mind drifts away from the mental image.

Practice this for one to two minutes.

For the third part, pick up the object and study it with your hands. Explore how it feels to touch the texture of the surfaces, the temperature, the edges, the feel of raised writing or scuff marks, etc. As you do this, continue to repeat your concentration cue when your mind wanders.

Practice this for one to two minutes.

Repeat this sequence several times a week. Notice how your ability to focus develops the more you practice it. You may even find that the practice becomes more and more relaxing and takes less and less effort to do.

Head to www.mentalitywins.com/resources for a downloadable Object Stare worksheet to help you practice this skill and evaluate your attentional progress.

PART 2

flow

establishing mindfulness

Jake was a competitive swimmer who crushed his times during practice but had started to struggle during high-stakes meets. As soon as he stepped onto the pool deck and heard the echo of his competitors' voices bouncing off the walls, his chest would tighten, and images of failure would flood into his mind. He'd see himself touching the wall in last place, and his teammates averting their eyes. Before he'd even dipped a toe in the water, something inside him had already decided he'd lost the race.

"I don't know what's wrong with me," he said to Jonathan. "I'm a really fast swimmer—my body can do incredible things. But put me in a competition, and my mind jumps straight to this nightmare scenario."

Jonathan recognized that Jake's problem wasn't physical—it was mental. Jake wasn't swimming the race he was in; he was swimming some other race that existed only in his mind. The trick was learning to ditch the imaginary race and engaging fully with the real one.

Jake and Jonathan worked together to integrate mindfulness into his routine, starting with breath awareness. Jake found that as long as he was focused on each breath, his mind couldn't spin off into the fantasies and predictions the way it used to. He also learned how to notice and name unhelpful thoughts instead of automatically accepting them as facts. When his mind said, I'm going to be dead last, *he learned to label it as simply a "thought" and let it go instead of getting sucked into the content and believing it as the truth.*

Slowly but surely, Jake began to stay fully present during his races. He realized that his lived reality was rarely as scary as the images in his mind. Indeed, the more present he became, the less anxious he was. By the end of the season, Jake had dropped 2.1 seconds off his 200-meter freestyle and qualified for championships in two events.

He told Jonathan, "The only thing I regret is not learning mindfulness years ago. I feel like I missed out on so much of my swimming career—but I'm finally here for every moment."

When Jake learned to practice mindfulness, he joined the ranks of elite athletes who have likewise discovered this game-changing tool. Kobe Bryant, for example, often credited his ability to stay calm and focused during high-pressure moments to his mindfulness practice.

Bryant's coach, Phil Jackson, was known as the "Zen Master" for incorporating mindfulness practices and Zen principles into team training. One of his most famous concepts was "One Breath, One Mind"—a phrase he used to describe how he wanted his team to be so completely present that all five players could move as a single thoughtful and tactical force.

Even though Jackson had three of the best players in NBA history on his teams (Shaquille O'Neal, Kobe Bryant, and Michael Jordan), his "One Breath, One Mind" philosophy empow-

ered other members of the team to go from glorified bystand-
ers to active participants in the team's success. Meanwhile, this
mindset freed the marquee players from feeling like they carried
sole responsibility for the team's success. As Jackson wrote in
his book *Sacred Hoops: Spiritual Lessons of a Hardwood Warrior*,
"Good teams become great when the members trust each other
enough to surrender the 'Me' for the 'We.'" By practicing mindfulness, the teams he coached developed the kind of trust in
themselves, in each other, and in life itself to let them perform
the quasi-miraculous.

Mindfulness is the practice of paying attention to the present moment without judgment—observing your thoughts, emotions, and physical sensations as they arise, without getting
caught up in them. For athletes, this means being aware of your
breathing, your body, your mentality, and the game—not the
score, the stakes, or the expectations.

Yet for many athletes, being fully present can feel almost impossible. You catch yourself calculating your final score when the
competition isn't even over yet, or wondering what your last move
is going to look like on video—or wondering if anyone caught it
on camera at all. You brace yourself for the next sprint instead
of running the mile you're in. You preview hundreds of different
scenarios in your mind, while forgetting where you are right now.

All this planning, rehearsing, and overthinking isn't a curse,
although it may feel that way sometimes. On the contrary, our
ability to analyze, evaluate, and anticipate the future is one of
the great gifts of human intelligence. But when you're trying to
stay present, that ability to think and plan can turn against you,
pulling your attention away from the moment you're trying to
inhabit as it unfolds.

Numerous studies show that mindfulness enhances athletic performance by sharpening attention, increasing present-

moment awareness, and boosting the perseverance required to overcome mistakes and other setbacks that occur during competition. Mindfulness doesn't make pressure disappear—but it does arm you with the skills you need to manage that pressure with confidence and clarity. Perhaps most importantly, mindfulness shifts you from obsessing over outcomes to embracing the process. Instead of looking too far ahead and getting lost in projections or fantasies, you put all your energy into what's happening right here, right now. That way, you can both access your full range of skills and experience genuine joy—no matter what the outcome of the competition may be.

THE LINK BETWEEN MINDFULNESS AND FLOW STATES

The *Tao Te Ching*, an ancient Chinese text attributed to the philosopher Lao Tzu, is an ode to the concept of *wu wei*, or "effortless action." In sixteenth century Japan, Zen Master Takuan Sōhō described a concept called *mushin*, or "no-mind," writing that it "travels about the entire body and extends itself throughout the entire self." And in ancient Greece, athletes experienced ecstasy when the Gods themselves seemed to flow through their bodies, making them capable of incredible feats.

Throughout human history, athletes, warriors, and artists have used many different names to describe the state of stillness, effortlessness, and bliss that can spontaneously arise when you are completely absorbed in your task. A certain kind of magic happens when you've put in the hard work of training and then let go of everything in a performance. These days, we call that state "flow."

Psychologist Mihaly Csikszentmihalyi coined the term "flow" in the 1970s. He defines it as a state of complete immersion in the present moment, when you're so absorbed in what you're doing that everything else disappears. When you're in flow, you're not thinking about what you just did or the play you're going to make next. You feel completely engaged but never overwhelmed. You have total control, yet it feels completely effortless. Your sense of self dissolves, time either speeds up or slows down, and playing becomes pure experience.

Athletes often refer to flow states as being "in the zone." Getting to experience a flow state is not an easy task—in fact, some people think of it as the holy grail of athletic performance, a sign that you've achieved true mastery. You need to have so many hours of practice behind you that you can shut off your thinking mind and rely solely on muscle memory and instinct. You need to be completely focused on the task at hand. And you need the mindfulness skills to truly *live* the moment instead of *thinking* about it.

As Kobe Bryant said about flow, "Nothing else is important other than what I am doing in this moment and time, and it's a beautiful feeling." Notice what Kobe emphasized: being present, accepting the moment, and not overthinking it. Those are the exact skills that mindfulness develops.

Mindfulness is a powerful gateway to flow because it trains your mind to do exactly what flow requires. It teaches you to stay present instead of getting pulled into the past or future. It helps you notice when your mind starts analyzing or judging, then gently brings your attention back to what's happening now. It builds your ability to observe thoughts and emotions without getting caught up in them.

When you practice mindfulness regularly, you're essentially rehearsing for flow. You're strengthening the mental muscles that allow you to drop into that state of complete presence where your best performances live. You're learning to trust the moment, accept whatever arises, and stay connected to the pure experience of playing your sport. Flow can't be forced, but it can be *invited*—and mindfulness is your invitation.

CORE MINDFULNESS SKILLS FOR ATHLETES

In the high-pressure world of sports, distractions are everywhere. Rumination about past mistakes, anxiety about future outcomes, and doubts about your abilities can cloud your focus and derail your performance. Mindfulness skills give you the tools to cut through that noise and bring your attention back to the things that really are within your control. The skills outlined below— breath awareness, body scanning, noticing and naming thoughts, gratitude, and savoring—are not quick fixes. They require commitment and practice. But for athletes willing to put in the effort, the payoff is immense. You will not only elevate your performance but also find greater joy and fulfillment in your sport.

Here are our favorite techniques for integrating mindfulness into your routine. We'll include specific exercises for each one at the end of this chapter.

BREATH AWARENESS

French Olympic swimmer and record holder Leon Marchand practices deep breathing every night as he falls asleep and uses this same breathing strategy on the blocks in a race to help him manage his energy for the competition. Thanks to his mindfulness practice, he says, "I feel capable of fighting with the best swimmers in the world. Before, I saw them as living gods. Now, I belong in this class of swimmers."

Marchand's example illustrates a profound truth: breath is one of the most powerful anchors to the present moment. Learning to focus on your breathing not only calms your nervous system but also gives you something to come back to when your mind wanders. When you breathe deep into your diaphragm—really filling your lungs from the bottom up—you're strengthening the same muscles that power your performance and teaching your body to take in oxygen more effectively. Every deep breath becomes an investment in your ability to last longer, push harder, and recover more quickly.

BODY SCANNING

Your body often holds tension in response to stress, even if you're not aware of it. A body scan is a mindfulness technique in which you slowly move your awareness through your body, identifying and releasing any areas of tension.

As renowned mindfulness researcher Jon Kabat-Zinn states in his book *Coming to Our Senses: Healing Ourselves and the World Through Mindfulness*, "If you think of your body as a musical instrument, the body scan is a way of tuning it. If you think of it as a universe, the body scan is a way to come to know it. If you think of your body as a house, the body scan is a way to throw open all the windows and doors and let the fresh air of awareness sweep it clean."

When you learn to pay attention to your bodily sensations at a finer and finer level, you not only become more present—you develop the kind of physical awareness that will help you become a master at your sport.

NOTICING AND NAMING
THOUGHTS AND EMOTIONS

Athletes often fall into the trap of believing every thought they have, especially the negative ones. Thoughts like "What if I miss this shot?" or "I'm not good enough" can quickly spiral into self-doubt and poor performance. Mindfulness teaches you to notice these thoughts and label them without judgment.

Psychiatrist Dan Siegel coined the expression "Name It to Tame It" to refer to the strategy of managing intense emotions by identifying them and labeling them. When you label a thought or emotion, it activates your left brain's language center, which then helps to regulate the more emotionally reactive right brain. By paying attention to the sensations and feelings associated with the emotion you've just labeled and noticing where you feel it in your body, you can understand it better and take its power away.

By labeling your thought or feeling, you create a bit of distance between you and it, which helps you avoid being consumed by it. Over time, this practice builds mental resilience. Naming your negative thoughts and emotions doesn't necessarily make them less uncomfortable, but it helps that discomfort be there without affecting your performance.

GRATITUDE

Oprah Winfrey once said, "Be thankful for what you have; you'll end up having more. If you concentrate on what you don't have, you will never, ever have enough." This nugget of wisdom expresses a deep truth about human psychology: where we direct our attention shapes our reality. When you pay attention to the things you cherish, you take it *away* from worries, judgments, and negative emotions.

At the end of each day or practice, take a moment to reflect on what you are grateful for—whether it's a small improvement in your game, a supportive teammate, or just the opportunity to compete. Make a point of expressing your gratitude instead of keeping it to yourself. This practice helps you stay grounded in the joy of your sport, even when the stakes are high. It also builds your anticipation of the next practice or game, as you frequently remember all the enjoyable aspects of your athletic life that motivate you to return to pursue greatness for another day.

SAVORING

The legendary golfer Ben Hogan once said, "As you walk down the fairway of life you must smell the roses, for you only get to play one round."

He was talking about savoring—the positive psychology practice of focusing your attention on enjoyable experiences and sensations, no matter how small they are.

We often go through our day either multitasking or distracted by thoughts and anxieties, rushing through many experiences that could otherwise be very pleasant or joyful. Savoring means hitting the pause button on those pleasant experiences so you can truly take them in—whether it's taking a good shot, making a good check, or laughing with your teammates on the bench. Instead of immediately moving on to the next thing, savoring teaches you to linger in those moments and take them in fully.

When you savor a positive experience, you extend its emotional impact and create happy memories that will buoy you through hard times. Think of it as squeezing every last drop out of the good moments in your life. Why rush past wonderful moments when you can linger in them?

The more you practice mindfulness in your everyday life, the more it will show up in your sport. Every mindful breath during morning practice, every moment of savoring a pregame meal with your teammates, and every time you neutrally observe your thoughts instead of reacting blindly to them, you're building the kind of present-moment awareness that unlocks true bliss and ease on the playing field.

SKILL TO TRY: 4-4-6 BREATHING

Before a high-pressure moment—a putt, a free throw, or stepping onto the field—take a few slow, intentional breaths. Inhale for four counts, hold for four, and exhale for six. This activates the parasympathetic nervous system, which helps regulate your stress response. The more you practice this in training, the more natural it will feel in competition.

SKILL TO TRY: BODY SCAN

Find a comfortable place to sit or lie down.

Start your body scan by paying attention to your feet. Inch by inch, slowly move your attention up your body: your heels, toes, top of the foot, ankles, calves, shins, knees, legs, thighs, buttocks, pelvis, abdomen, hips, back, chest, shoulders, arms, neck, throat, jaw, cheeks, nose, ears, eyes, temples, ending with the top of your head.

As you scan, observe the sensations you feel in each body part without judgment. Release any tension you encounter using your breath.

Once you complete the body scan, take a moment to feel your entire body as a whole and then slowly bring your attention to the present.

SKILL TO TRY: THOUGHT CONVEYOR BELT

Imagine your thoughts are items coming down a conveyor belt, and your job is to stick an accurate and descriptive label on each one.

For example, if you have the thought, *I'm choking*, you might label the thought as "anxiety about performance" or simply "nerves." If you have the thought, *I just don't know how I'm going to make it to the end of the game*, you might label it "worry."

How does your relationship to your thoughts change when you label them in a calm and neutral way?

SKILL TO TRY: GRATITUDE BOOSTERS

Here are three simple ways to incorporate a gratitude practice into your daily life:

- Keep a gratitude jar in your room. Each time you think of it, write something you are grateful for on a small piece of paper, fold it up, and put it in the jar. Over time, the jar will start to fill up, and on days when you are feeling down or need a boost, you can reach your hand in, unfold one of the pieces of paper, and read it to yourself and reflect on it.

- Use a gratitude rock: Find a rock that has a smooth or interesting texture that you can hold on to while you intentionally reflect on the things you are grateful for. By combining your sense of touch with your thankful thoughts, you will further solidify the gratitude you feel.

- Make a gratitude box: Get a shoe box where you can put items that remind you of people, places, and things you are grateful for. From time to time, or as you need it, spend a few minutes going through some of the items in the box and pay attention to the positive emotions you feel as you look at them.

SKILL TO TRY: SIMPLE WAYS TO SAVOR

Here are some simple ideas to make savoring a part of your daily life:

- Savor your pregame meal by eating slowly, thinking about how good it tastes, focusing on the flavor and texture of the food, and reflecting on how it's going to fuel you for competition.

- Look at a photo of you or your team playing your sport. Allow yourself to feel the joy, pride, and other positive emotions you see in the picture. See if you can bring yourself back to how it felt to be competing in the moment, in body and mind.

- Savor the athletic arena. The next time you are on the field, court, track, rink, or other athletic environment, take a moment to really appreciate your surroundings. Smell the smells, see the sights, and really try to savor every aspect of the environment where you train and compete.

Head to www.mentalitywins.com/resources for a list of ways to savor your day and create more moments of gratitude and enjoyment, both in and out of sport.

mastering uncertainty

Amanda was a talented hockey player with a big problem: she couldn't handle the unpredictable nature of her sport. Her coach sent her to Kim because she had explosive reactions to anything that went wrong: missed shots, questionable referee calls, and personal mistakes. She'd yell at teammates, berate referees until she earned penalties, and slam her stick so hard against the boards that she once broke it in half. In a sport where split-second decisions, human error, and subjective officiating are constants, Amanda was fighting a battle she couldn't win: trying to control the uncontrollable.

"I know it's not okay to blow up at people," she told Kim. "But it just frustrates me so much when I see a teammate doing something wrong or making a bad play, I wish I could grab the stick out of her hands and do it myself."

Kim's work with Amanda focused on developing what they called "uncertainty tolerance"—the ability to stay cool and collected when things don't go according to plan. Amanda learned that even though she couldn't control all the variables of the game, she could still decide how to respond to them. When she felt the physical tingle that came with uncertainty, she trained herself to interpret it as a sign of excitement and possibility, not a looming threat.

The turning point came during a crucial game when Amanda's teammate passed the puck directly to the opposing team, leading to a goal. Instead of her usual explosive reaction, Amanda took a reset breath, skated over to her teammate, and said, "Shake it off—we'll get the next one." Her teammate later told the coach it was the first time Amanda had ever supported her after a mistake.

By season's end, Amanda had transformed from the team's most volatile player into one of its most reliable leaders. Her penalty minutes dropped by 70 percent, and her teammates started confiding in her instead of avoiding her.

Amanda's journey illustrates the extraordinary power of mastering uncertainty in sports. No matter which sport you're competing in, you're going to face multiple types of uncertainty throughout the season. For starters, there's physical uncertainty: you never know if your body is going to perform at its peak on any given day, especially during a grueling playoff or tournament. There's also competitive uncertainty, as your competitors will always surprise you with new strategies, and your own teammates will make unpredictable mistakes. Most athletes also deal with environmental uncertainty, like unpredictable weather, variable ice and snow conditions, and factors like air pollution. Finally, you have surprise curveballs like injuries, accidents, and questionable calls by referees.

Have you ever shown up to a game or competition, only to feel a sense of dread, despair, or outrage when things aren't quite how you expected? Have you ever found yourself thinking things like, *How are we supposed to race in this wind?* or *Who's that new player on the other team?* Even though you may know on an intellectual level that you can't control every little thing about your sport, it can still feel like a personal affront when things don't look the way you imagined. Maybe, like Amanda, the fear you feel in moments of uncertainty has been hampering your game.

Athletes who thrive in moments of uncertainty have a huge advantage. They can adapt to whatever the competition throws at them while deploying the full range of their technical and tactical skills. They can stay emotionally balanced even when things feel overwhelming, outrageous, or unfair. And even though they might *feel* worried or angry, they don't let those emotions get in the way of executing the game plan. When you get good at rolling with uncertainty, you'll realize that some of your proudest moments and most brilliant plays came from handling things you didn't expect. After all, if every basketball game, gymnastics routine, or snowboard jump went exactly according to plan, why would anyone bother watching?

Making peace with uncertainty frees you up to be fully present, completely engaged with what is instead of stuck on ideas of what should be—and these are exactly the ingredients you need to enter flow states. When Amanda stopped fighting the unpredictability of hockey and learned to embrace it, she didn't just become a better teammate—she also started experiencing more of those magical moments when the game felt easy, natural, and joyful. Mastering uncertainty doesn't *guarantee* flow states, but it removes one of the biggest obstacles standing in their way.

UNCERTAINTY FEELS HARD
FOR A REASON

Uncertainty automatically creates stress and anxiety in the brain—at least until you train your brain to respond to uncertainty in a new way. This is because the human brain is a prediction machine, always trying to anticipate what's coming next so you can get ready for it. When you don't know what's going to happen, or when something happens that you weren't counting on, your brain can go into fight-or-flight mode, flooding your body with hormones like cortisol and adrenaline. Your muscles tense, your heart rate shoots up, and your attention narrows. All of these reactions can get in the way of the precise motor skills and clear decision-making your sport requires.

Another useful-but-unfortunate feature of our brains is that they have a built-in negativity bias when facing uncertainty. When we don't know what's going to happen, we tend to imagine the worst-case scenario rather than considering neutral or positive possibilities. Instead of thinking, *This could go really well*, we jump straight to *Holy crap, this is* never *going to work.* Although negativity bias can be helpful in a genuine survival situation where you need to consider every possible danger, it's not so useful on the field or in the arena, where those negative projections can kill confidence and stamp out creativity.

The more uncertainty there is in a particular game or match, the more mental energy your brain burns trying to figure things out. Let's say there's a heat wave, you're dealing with an unexpected injury, and your opponent has come up with a bewildering new play you've never seen before. If you let the uncertainty intimidate you, your brain will run wild trying to "solve" every variable and gain some semblance of control. This leaves fewer cognitive resources available for the tasks that *really* matter, like reading the defense, making split-second decisions, or executing precise physical movements. It's like trying to solve a complex math problem while someone is talking loudly on their cell phone nearby—it's technically possible, but much harder than it needs to be.

In a nutshell: uncertainty feels hard because it *is* hard. But if uncertainty didn't exist, there would be no point in playing sports. Think about how boring it would be if every day had perfect weather, every shot and pass and throw was executed perfectly, and every player could perfectly predict their opponent's next move. Who would want to watch that? There'd be no emotion, no tension, no excitement, no sense of pride or fulfillment—no hard-won victories at all.

The answer isn't to try to eliminate all uncertainty from sport—this simply can't be done. What you need to do instead is rewire your response to uncertainty, learning to see it as a necessary, exciting, and desirable component of sport instead of a flaw to be eliminated.

Think of a time when uncertainty propelled you to a new level of mastery. Maybe you showed up to snowboard and found that the slope was covered in ice, you had to learn to pitch a baseball with a sprained finger, or you arrived at your weekly tennis match only to be paired with an opponent you weren't expecting. Even though you might have felt a little nervous or daunted at first, by the end of the session you probably uncovered some creative adaptability you didn't even realize you had. Maybe you even went on to *crave* uncertainty, enjoying the new challenges it presented to you.

THE INDIVIDUAL ZONES OF OPTIMAL FUNCTIONING

Every athlete needs just the right amount of activation to perform their best—the right number of butterflies in your stomach or tingle in your hands. If you have *too* much activation, it can tip into fear, panic, or even choking. And if you have too *little* activation, you might not feel the buzz you need to lock in.

In the 1970s, the sport psychologist Yuri Hanin developed the Individual Zones of Optimal Functioning (IZOF) model to describe the way that each individual athlete has a "sweet spot" for activation—it's not one-size-fits-all. Some athletes play their best when they're absolutely terrified, while others can only perform well when they're deeply relaxed.

The IZOF model explains why some athletes play their best when competing against tough opponents but lose when they're matched up against easier competition. An athlete who thrives in high-pressure games needs a higher level of arousal (aka anxiety and nervousness) to play their best. When you put them in a low-stress situation, they feel too relaxed or even bored to do a good job.

Here's where uncertainty comes in: When something unpredictable happens during competition, you have a choice in how you frame it. If you interpret that uncertainty as a threat, your activation level will spike, potentially pushing you out of your optimal zone. But if you interpret that same uncertainty as an interesting challenge or opportunity, you can maintain or adjust your activation to stay within your sweet spot.

Think of the physical sensations that come along with uncertainty: tingling, butterflies, a faster heartbeat, maybe clenched muscles or sweaty palms. Often, our knee-jerk response is to interpret those sensations as a sign that we're in danger. But when you think about happy or exciting moments in your life—say, the moment before your first kiss or before opening your college acceptance letter—you'll realize you had many of the same sensations. The difference is, you *interpreted* them as a sign that something exciting was about to happen, not as a source of dread.

By consciously choosing how you interpret uncertainty, you can steer yourself toward your performance sweet spot and stay there. Athletes who master this skill essentially gain a volume knob for their nervous system, allowing them to turn their activation up or down as needed to stay in their zone. As Steph

Curry says, "I've never been afraid of big moments. I get nervous and anxious, but I think those are all good signs that I'm ready for the moment."

CHOKING

Learning to reframe uncertainty is a powerful skill, but sometimes, despite our best efforts, things can still go wrong. When uncertainty triggers too much activation and pushes you too far outside your optimal zone, you can end up in territory that every athlete dreads. Your carefully practiced skills seem to vanish, your body stops responding the way it should, and instead of rising to the challenge, you're paralyzed. This experience has a name that strikes fear into the hearts of athletes everywhere: choking.

If you've ever choked—and most athletes have—you know the list of symptoms well. As your activation level spiraled upward, your brain scrambled to reestablish control, desperately looking for ways to "get back on track." You probably experienced a fractured sense of self as you struggled to reconcile the athlete you knew yourself to be with the quivering wreck you seemed to be now—and you might have felt rising panic as the skills you've spent literally thousands of hours practicing seemed to desert you just when you needed them most.

Choking isn't just painful in the moment—the distress can linger long after the original event. It's common to feel ashamed, confused, and like your trust in yourself has been shaken. Even if you've been an elite player for years, you may find yourself avoiding games and competitions out of fear of choking again—and even when you *do* play, you might spend more and more mental energy on the task of "avoiding choking," leaving less left over to play your best. If being an athlete is a big part of your identity, the fear of choking can have devastating consequences not only on your game but also on your mental health.

Kim has experienced choking several times as a new golfer. Most often, this occurs when she either rushes the shot or gives herself too much time to think. Notice that *both* of these behaviors are attempts to limit uncertainty. When you rush, you're essentially trying to escape the discomfort of not knowing what will happen. Your brain says, "I can't stand to hang out at this level of activation—let's just get it over with and hope it works!" The irony is that by rushing to escape uncertainty, you often guarantee a worse outcome because you don't give yourself the chance to execute properly.

On the flip side, when you overthink, that's your brain trying to eliminate uncertainty through sheer mental effort, as if thinking hard enough will somehow make the outcome predictable. But most sports require a balance between conscious thinking and unconscious execution. When you try to consciously control movements that should be automatic, you disrupt the very muscle memory you've spent so long developing.

To reduce her chance of choking, Kim approaches her putts the same way every time. She always marks her ball, even if it's a putt she feels she could sink easily. She also reminds herself that the more she practices putting, the more confident she becomes, which makes choking in the future less likely. Perhaps most importantly, she knows how to manage her activation level by reframing the physical sensations that go along with uncertainty.

Choking less means drawing a bright line between the things you can control and the things you can't. This mental discipline stops your mind from wasting energy trying to control the uncontrollable. Practicing specific skills like free throws and short putts until they become second nature is another effective antidote because they mean you can rely on your body and muscle memory even when your mind is overwhelmed. And if you want to take it even further, you can deeply accept the fact that choking—as uncomfortable as it may be—is part and parcel of playing sports.

If you've developed a fear of choking that is emotionally crippling or stopping you from enjoying your sport, you may benefit from working with a mental skills coach or a sport clinician. These professionals can help you delve into the potential causes for choking under pressure or mismanaging uncertainty during competition, and help you develop strategies for meeting those challenges.

THE ACCEPTANCE AND COMMITMENT APPROACH TO UNCERTAINTY

One of the most effective treatments for choking and general fear of uncertainty is Acceptance and Commitment Therapy (ACT). This technique helps break you out of the patterns that reinforce negative thinking, cognitive cloudiness, and negative emotions. ACT teaches that emotional challenges don't come from the events themselves but from the way we interpret those events. For example, you could see an incident of choking as a sign that you're a terrible athlete, or you could see it as a sign that you got pushed outside your IZOF and learn techniques to stay within it.

ACT teaches that instead of trying to make anxiety go away, you can instead accept that anxiety is a normal part of performing at a high level. Not only does everyone get nervous, but getting nervous doesn't necessarily mean you're going to choke or perform poorly, as research on the IZOF shows. In fact, sometimes our very best performances happen when we are quivering in the starting gate just moments before!

Accepting that uncomfortable emotions like anxiety are normal and not necessarily harmful gives you incredible freedom. Instead of wasting energy trying to force your emotions to change, you can focus on the next play. You can remind yourself that your teammates have your back in competition, that you have hours of training behind you, and that anxiety is just a feeling, not an accurate prediction of future events.

USING MENTAL REHEARSAL AND VISUALIZATION

Once you've accepted uncertainty as a normal and even desirable aspect of sports, and gotten into the habit of reframing it in a positive light, what else can you do to prepare for it? Two techniques we recommend to athletes all the time are mental rehearsal and visualization.

Mental rehearsal means imagining challenging or high-pressure situations in order to prepare for them in competition. For example, if you're a sprinter, you might mentally rehearse the steps you'd take in the event of a false start in the 100-meter final. You'd imagine hearing the recall gun, feeling your frustration and other emotions, resetting mentally, then exploding out of the blocks cleanly on your second attempt. If you're a gymnast, you might mentally rehearse what to do if you lose your grip and fall off the uneven bars mid-routine, imagining yourself landing safely, remounting with confidence, and finishing the rest of your routine strong.

Mentally rehearsing surprises like these reduces their shock factor. By allowing your mind to preview the stressors of competition, your psyche can be better prepared when those moments present themselves in real life. It's like a preflight safety check where pilots review their roles and responsibilities for potential emergencies. By running through these procedures *before* the plane takes off, pilots can respond effectively if a real crisis arises and their cognitive resources are stretched thin. In the same way, mental rehearsal lets you map out exactly how you want to handle high-pressure moments before you're dealing with a flood of stress and adrenaline.

In contrast, **visualization** is the practice of imagining a successful rep or movement. Even though it's called visualization, it's not just about the eyes—ideally, you should use all your senses to recreate the sensations of your sport as faithfully as possible. For example, you can imagine yourself making the perfect free throw, feeling the texture of the ball against your fingers and hearing the swoosh when it goes in the net.

Visualization lets you continue to practice long after it would be unhealthy for your physical body to do so. For example, a softball pitcher can visualize herself facing one hundred different batters, but the same pitcher's body would break down if she tried to do the same thing in real life. As your brain rehearses your sport, it treats these imagined events as real experiences, strengthening mind-body connections and deepening your understanding of movement patterns and strategy.

When you visualize yourself performing in different conditions—rain, wind, hot sun, slippery course, clever competitors—you can get out ahead of uncertainty because you've already prepared for it in your mind. When you show up to an event, you're far less likely to get thrown off, because you've already practiced handling all kinds of different situations. You have real practice performing under all sorts of conditions, and your brain doesn't care that it's "only" imaginary.

Mastering uncertainty isn't about becoming fearless or eliminating all the butterflies in your stomach—it's about changing your relationship with the unknown. When you stop seeing uncertainty as the enemy and start seeing it as a necessary element that makes sports exciting, you free up enormous amounts of mental energy. Instead of burning cognitive fuel trying to control every variable, you can channel that energy into the things that actually matter: reading the game, making smart decisions, and being there for your team.

SKILL TO TRY: REFRAMING UNCERTAINTY

When uncertainty hits during competition, try reframing your emotions as excitement instead of fear or anxiety. See it as an opportunity to lean on your preparedness to conquer a new obstacle. For example, instead of telling yourself, "This wasn't supposed to happen," tell yourself, "I'm prepared for this." Instead of "I don't know how to handle this," tell yourself, "I will figure out how to handle this." Remind yourself that physical sensations like butterflies in your stomach aren't signs of danger, but signals that your body is ready to perform.

With practice, you will start to experience the physiological sensations that go along with uncertainty as a sign that something interesting or exciting is going to happen, not something bad or wrong.

Head to www.mentalitywins.com/resources for a list of responses you can say to yourself when encountering uncertainty to help shift yourself from anxiety to excitement.

teamwork and peak performance

Marcus was a twenty-two-year-old swimmer on the national adaptive swim team who had been the anchor of his team's relay for three years. Marcus had cerebral palsy and had worked incredibly hard to earn his spot as the team's most reliable swimmer in the 100-meter freestyle. His confidence came not just from his times but from being the teammate everyone looked up to—the vet who mentored new swimmers and kept team morale high during tough training blocks.

His world came crashing down on the day Suresh joined the team. Suresh wasn't just fast—he immediately posted times that threatened Marcus's position on the relay—he was also charismatic, funny, and seemed to effortlessly connect with teammates with whom it had taken Marcus years to build relationships. Seemingly overnight, teammates started gravitating toward Suresh during breaks, asking him for advice, and even sitting with him instead of Marcus during team meals.

Marcus came to Jonathan feeling confused and ashamed about his reaction to Suresh. "I should be happy for the team," he told Jonathan. "We're faster with Suresh, and he's a great person. But I can't stop feeling like I'm being replaced. I've been working toward making the Paralympic team for five years, and now I'm worried I won't get a spot. Worse, I catch myself hoping that Suresh will have a bad practice or get injured, and then I hate myself for having those thoughts."

Jonathan worked with Marcus to help him understand that his feelings were completely normal. Together, they explored how Marcus's identity had become deeply intertwined with being "the best" and "the leader," and how Suresh's arrival was challenging not just his athletic position but his sense of self-worth. Jonathan helped Marcus focus on what he could control: his training, his attitude, and his choice to be a good teammate.

He also encouraged Marcus to accept Suresh's presence instead of shying away from him or resisting the change. He began working with Suresh on relay handoffs, sharing insights about race strategy, and even suggesting that they co-lead team meetings. Rather than trying to rein in Suresh's influence, Marcus found ways to work with it. By the end of the season, Marcus and Suresh had developed a partnership that made the whole team stronger.

Marcus not only made the Paralympic team but also swam some of his best times ever. His jealousy of Suresh never completely disappeared, but Marcus developed the skills to notice those feelings without letting them drive his behavior, allowing him to be both competitive and genuinely supportive of his teammates' achievements.

No matter how much you love your team, you're bound to experience tension every now and then. Whether it's conflicting personalities, shifting dynamics when a new player comes in, competition for playing time, or toxic attitudes like racism, classism, or homophobia, sports teams can be hotbeds of conflict *and* seedbeds for rapid personal growth.

Think about how much time you spend with your teammates. Between practices, games, travel, team meals, and casual hangouts outside of sports, you might be spending more waking hours with these people than with your own family. When your team functions well, all those hours become incredibly enriching. You're not just getting better at your sport; you're building friendships, learning how to work with different personalities, and creating memories that will last long after your days as a competitive athlete are over. But in some cases, like Marcus experienced, you might find yourself in competition with your own teammates, not just with opposing teams—a particularly raw and sensitive situation. And when team dynamics go wrong, all that time together can become a toxic chemical bath of stress, jealousy, and insecurity.

Jonathan once played on a lacrosse team with a culture of racial intolerance. Before Jonathan joined the team, the players used to make racist comments on a regular basis. Although they toned it down now that there were Black players on the team, some jokes and comments still slipped out. It was hard to feel like his teammates had his best interests in mind or had his back during games. When he confronted his teammates about their behavior, they would provide any and all excuses. Jonathan loved his sport but felt so insulted and conflicted that he wasn't sure if he could stay.

The issue came to a head when the Black players confronted the White players, who were responsible for the majority of the comments. It escalated into a heated argument. In the aftermath, the whole team had a meeting to discuss the impacts of the racist comments and attitudes. In response, the players who were making the comments voluntarily left the team, and the remaining teammates began the process of repair. This led the team to have more success on the field and more unity off of it, although things never truly returned to normal.

Even positive team experiences can bring complicated emotions to the surface. Sometimes the hardest team moments aren't about conflict or toxicity at all—they're about navigating competing loyalties, managing disappointment, or simply feeling the weight of caring deeply about things you can't always control.

Midway through the hockey season of Kim's Junior year at Harvard, it was becoming clear that her team had a real chance at the National Championship. Then, four of their best players announced that they would be missing a weekend of games to go compete for their countries in the World Championship. As they sat together in the locker room during the team discussion, heavy emotions hung in the air. Kim remembers that she and her teammates said to the players leaving to play in the Worlds, "This is *our* Olympics." This wasn't about convincing their teammates not to go—it was about expressing to them how much they would be missed in this crucial weekend.

Even as they mourned their teammates' absence, Kim's team didn't let this unexpected setback derail them. They stayed focused and won their weekend games. Meanwhile, the Olympians came back having grown from the experience of playing internationally and were excited to rejoin the team on their journey to the National Championship. The reunion was joyful and energizing. Facing this uncertainty together not only reinvigorated the team but also gave less-experienced players the chance to step up in the star players' absence, instilling a new sense of confidence within the entire core of the team.

Team sports expose us to the full spectrum of human emotions and relationships—sometimes all within the same season.

Kim's story shows how teams can navigate disappointment and uncertainty with grace, turning potential division into an opportunity for growth. Jonathan's experience, on the other hand, shows how toxic attitudes can poison the entire team environment and force difficult but necessary confrontations. His story demonstrates that sometimes healthy team culture means taking a stand, even when it's uncomfortable or risky.

THE CONNECTION BETWEEN TEAMWORK AND FLOW

Even though we tend to think of flow states as an individual experience, the truth is your teammates and team culture play a crucial role in helping you access flow. If you have total trust in your teammates and feel trusted by them in return, you'll feel much more confident letting go, sinking into the present moment, and entering a flow state. However, if you feel that your teammates don't have your back or simply can't be trusted to do their jobs, your mental energy will go into trying to manage those fears and distractions. With this in mind, laying the groundwork for flow states really is a team endeavor, not a lone pursuit.

If you ever watched the Chicago Bulls or LA Lakers when Phil Jackson was coach, you know what it's like to watch a whole team enter a flow state together: moments of breathtaking harmony where each player seems to know exactly where their teammate is going to be, to the point that they can make passes without even glancing to make sure the player is really there. These players not only had elite skills on an individual level—they were intimately connected to each other, with a deeply supportive team culture.

But even if you're in a more individual sport like gymnastics or track and field, your teammates still have a dramatic impact on your ability to enter a flow state. Even if you're performing alone, the support you feel from your teammates, the trust you have in your coaches, and the psychological safety your team has created will all impact your ability to lock in and let go.

Teams that nurture flow states share several characteristics. First, they communicate openly and constructively instead of letting things like resentment and jealousy simmer. Second, they celebrate each other's successes genuinely, giving props where props are due. They handle mistakes with support and encouragement instead of blame, cultivating the feeling that everyone has each other's back. Finally, they create an environment where taking risks feels safe instead of threatening.

When your team environment supports flow, you'll notice that your individual performances feel more effortless, creative, and joyful. You'll take risks you might not take otherwise, knowing your teammates will be there for you regardless of the outcome. You'll find yourself less distracted by external pressures because you're anchored in the trust and connection you feel with your team. Most excitingly, you'll discover that your own flow states become contagious, helping lift your teammates to their own peak performances and creating an upward spiral of getting in the zone.

Of course, building this kind of supportive team culture isn't always simple. While the ideal team creates conditions for flow, the reality is that teams are made up of individuals with their own needs, ambitions, weaknesses, and priorities. Even the most cohesive teams, with the healthiest cultures, still face tensions that can threaten that all-important psychological safety and trust. Understanding these tensions—and learning to navigate them skillfully—is essential for maintaining the team dynamics that make flow possible.

MANAGING CONFLICTING GOALS

One of the biggest sources of team tension happens when players' personal goals put them at odds with team goals. For example, you might be pursuing the team goal of winning the championship, but at the same time, you might also be competing with certain teammates for a scarce resource like a college scholarship or more playing time. Pursuing both these goals at once creates tension that can be tricky to navigate, even for the most emotionally intelligent players.

For example, let's say you're one of two point guards on your basketball team, and you're both hoping to land a college scholarship—a feat that depends on individual stats and playing time. This can create all kinds of mental quandaries. Should you make that extra pass or take the shot yourself to boost your personal stats? Should you do whatever you can to vie for those precious extra minutes on the court, even when it means edging out your teammate? How do you balance your need to land that coveted scholarship with the needs of the team as a whole? These aren't easy questions, and there's rarely a perfect answer.

One good approach is to ask yourself, "Could I justify this decision to my coach, my teammates, and myself without feeling ashamed?" If you take a reasonable shot that happens to improve your stats, the answer is probably yes. If you force a questionable shot because you're trying to juice up your numbers, it will probably be obvious to everyone—scouts included. If you have a decent and honest justification for your decisions during games and competitions, you'll find the right balance between supporting your teammates and pursuing the goals you hold dear.

It's also important to keep things in context. Notice when you're getting hung up on one factor—such as stats or playing time—and ignoring other elements that are pertinent to your goal, such as maturity, self-control, deep knowledge of the game, and coachability. Notice, too, when you're slipping into a scarcity mindset that tells you there isn't enough to go around and that if you don't get *this* exact opportunity, you're finished. Even though competition for spots and scholarships is very real, catastrophizing about any one outcome is going to make you lose sight of all the other paths to success. Yes, it's possible that you won't get a scholarship to School A—but you might get one to School B, and you might thrive there.

Finally, remind yourself that your teammates are experiencing the same inner conflict as you—you're not alone in feeling this strain. *Everyone* wants to get their dream scholarship, their dream playing time, and their dream spot on an elite team, and everyone is going to feel sadness, disappointment, and frustration if they don't get it. Wrestling with these difficult emotions doesn't make you unique—it's the norm. Can you become the person on your team who recognizes the shared struggle instead of making it all about you?

When everyone on your team can acknowledge the difficulty while supporting each other anyway, a powerful force emerges: psychological safety.

PSYCHOLOGICAL SAFETY

Psychological safety, a term coined by Harvard Business School professor Amy Edmondson, refers to a team culture in which every player can speak up, ask questions, admit mistakes, and be vulnerable without fear of retaliation or shaming. Teams with strong psychological safety perform better than teams where the players feel like they're on thin ice. This is because when you have psychological safety, you're more willing to take risks and be vulnerable. When players feel safe to experiment with new techniques and communicate openly about what they're feeling and experiencing, the whole team benefits.

The 1996 Chicago Bulls are an example of a team whose coach established a culture of both athletic excellence and psychological well-being. Coach Phil Jackson knew that it wasn't enough to have dazzling technical skills—for his team to truly be unstoppable, the players also needed trust and vulnerability. This atmosphere of psychological safety meant that the team could draw on a deep well of resilience in situations that would otherwise be emotionally crushing.

Jackson's star player, Michael Jordan, embodied the team's values of accountability, integrity, and tremendous effort. When his teammates saw him working diligently and being held to a high standard by their coach, they knew that they too needed to put great work into their craft and that they couldn't just let Mike do everything. The '96 Bulls didn't just rely on talent—they also called upon their deep self-knowledge, shared goals, and tremendous trust they had in each other to do the work and be there for each other.

As a team member, you can help create psychological safety by modeling the behavior you want to see. Admit when you don't understand something, ask for help when you're struggling, and acknowledge when you make mistakes. When teammates see that being vulnerable doesn't lead to getting punished or shamed, it gives them permission to do the same. These small acts of courage can gradually shift the entire team culture.

Another way you can contribute to psychological safety is by calling people in instead of calling them out, a phrase made popular by Smith College professor and civil rights activist Loretta J. Ross. Instead of publicly embarrassing someone for mistakes, bad behavior, or displays of negative emotion, pull them aside and talk to them one-on-one. For example, you could say, "Hey,

I noticed you seemed frustrated during that drill. Everything okay?" This approach encourages teammates to open up to you instead of resenting you for calling them out.

You can also have regular team check-ins where everyone can share how they're feeling about practices, games, or team dynamics. Having preplanned, low-stress opportunities for honest communication makes it easier for teammates to speak up, instead of feeling like the onus is on them to initiate a hard conversation.

PRO TIPS FOR BUILDING STRONG TEAMS

Building a strong team culture requires intentional effort by everyone on the team. Even though coaches and captains play a big role in setting the tone, the truth is that every player contributes to the vibe, whether or not they realize it. Here are some concrete ways you can help build a strong culture for your team:

CELEBRATE YOUR TEAMMATES' SUCCESSES.

University of Alabama softball coach Patrick Murphy teaches his players the Buddhist concept of *mudita*. Mudita is a Sanskrit term that means "sympathetic joy"—the practice of delighting in the achievements of others, rather than stewing in envy or jealousy. When you embrace this mentality, you can celebrate your teammates' successes wholeheartedly instead of worrying about how their excellent performance reflects on you. As Murphy says, "If you can be as happy for your teammates' success as if you did it yourself, the sky's the limit."

DON'T LET PINCHES TURN INTO CRUNCHES.

Lee-J Mirasolo, head coach of the Stonehill College Women's Hockey team, has all the players on her team read the book *Connect* by David Bradford and Carole Robin so they can all develop a common language to talk about conflict. One idea from the book is "pinches and crunches." Pinches are minor moments of hurt or disappointment that we may not always voice—but if left to fester, they can build into crunches, which are serious beefs or open conflicts.

Lee-J encourages her team members to address pinches by expressing their feelings before the pinch grows into a crunch. This gives the person who (often unknowingly) hurt their teammate a chance to change their behavior.

ASK FOR HELP.

If you're experiencing a serious violation such as bullying or racism, or struggling with a concern like feeling left out or overshadowed, don't suffer in silence. Talk to your team captain, coach, athletic director, or someone not involved with the team at all, such as a psychologist or counselor. Most importantly, don't buy into the toxic idea that "what happens in the locker room stays in the locker room." After all, if you put up with abusive treatment from others, you're paving the way for the players who come after you to receive that treatment as well.

Team sports are always going to stretch you in ways that individual hobbies simply can't. You'll face moments like Marcus did, where someone else's success feels like a threat to your own dreams. You'll navigate situations like Kim's team experienced,

where competing loyalties create disappointment—and opportunities. And you might find yourself in Jonathan's position, forced to choose between staying quiet and taking a stand
against unacceptable behavior. These challenges force you to
develop the emotional intelligence, conflict resolution skills,
and moral courage that will serve you for the rest of your life.

SKILL TO TRY:
DAILY TEAMMATE CHECK-IN

Pick one teammate each day and make a genuine effort to connect with them beyond just sports talk. Ask how they're doing,
notice if they seem off, or simply acknowledge something they
did well in practice. This could be as simple as "Great hustle on
that drill today" or "You seem quieter than usual—everything
okay?" These small moments of connection build the trust and
psychological safety that help teams play their best.

PART 3

finish

building resilience

Dave was a pitcher who gave up a three-run, game-tying home run late in the eighth inning of his baseball team's playoff game. Not only was he booed by his home crowd, but his teammates showed their displeasure with contemptuous body language and disgusted looks on their faces. As his opponent jogged around the bases, a wave of utter humiliation swept over him. He let himself feel it for a few seconds—but then he made a choice.

Standing on the mound, he took three deep breaths and reminded himself of what Kim had taught him in their sessions: to let go of failures quickly and focus on the next move. Doing a quick mental scan, he realized he'd had the wrong grip on the ball—a mechanical issue he could fix on the next pitch.

Dave struck out the next batter looking and got the next to hit a lazy fly ball to center field to end the inning. His team rallied in the bottom of the ninth, scoring two runs to win the game.

After the game, his coach patted him on the back. "Dave, a lot of players would have let that moment crush them. But you dusted yourself off and conducted yourself with dignity. I'm proud of you."

Dave went home that night feeling good about himself. His skills at managing tough moments served him well throughout the rest of the season, and he went on to become his team's MVP.

———

Have you ever walked off the court or playing field after a crushing loss, replaying every mistake and wondering if you'll ever be able to shake this horrible defeat from your mind? That knot in your chest, the unenthusiastic hugs and handshakes from teammates, the quiet car ride home with your family, and the self-doubt running reckless in your mind? Believe it or not, these raw and painful moments are the seed from which resilience springs.

You don't build resilience from easy wins or games where everything goes your way. You build it by sitting with discomfort and making a conscious choice about what comes next. Those awful feelings you experience after a setback are the raw material that builds mental toughness—*if* you know how to work with them skillfully. In the moments after you fumble the ball or miss the shot, you have a choice: you can either wallow in shame and frustration, or you can shift your focus to whatever comes next.

Resilience is the skill of bouncing back from the difficult moments that go along with being an athlete—the injuries, defeats, embarrassments, and everyday stressors of training and competing. Sports are rightfully celebrated for their ability to build resilience—indeed, this is often why parents push their kids to join a baseball team or play soccer. The mental toughness you build on the field follows you into job interviews, relationship struggles, and everything else life throws your way. But building resilience isn't something you finish doing as a child or teenager—it's a lifelong process. As an athlete, every setback you encounter is an opportunity to hone this crucial skill, no matter how long you've been involved with your sport.

Most people throw around the word "resilience" without really understanding what it means. At its core, resilience boils down to two simple things. First, it means going through a challenging experience and coming out stronger—not just surviving, but growing from it. Second, resilience means getting better at handling stress. This means learning how to stay calm, keep your head on your shoulders, and take thoughtful, appropriate action when everything around you and within you feels chaotic.

You can't build resilience by avoiding stress. As Viktor Frankl, the founder of logotherapy and Holocaust survivor famously said, "What [a person] actually needs is not a tensionless state but rather the striving and struggling for a goal worthy of [them]." In other words, we thrive not when our lives are easy and comfortable, but when we have something worth fighting for—something that engages us at the deepest level and pushes us to grow.

This wisdom flies in the face of how most of us *think* we want to live. We rarely daydream about stress and difficulty. Instead, we fantasize about smooth sailing, easy wins, and everything going exactly to plan. Yet in order to become a more resilient athlete, you *must* be exposed to difficult situations, both in and out of sport. You can't learn how to handle pressure by reading about it or watching someone else go through it. You have to face a situation in which you're forced to discover that skill within yourself.

The challenging moments you encounter as an athlete force you to get creative—and getting creative helps you discover new strategies you might have never otherwise learned. For example, let's say you're a boxer who's about to face the tallest opponent in your gym. Yes, it's intimidating—this person has six inches on you! But if you lean into the challenge, you might learn how to use speed and footwork to neutralize the reach advantage, and this will serve you well in future matches. If instead, you had declined to face that particular opponent, you would have missed the opportunity to make this discovery.

Every time you face a tough situation and figure out how to work through it, you're adding a layer to your mental armor. There are *always* reasons to want to run and hide or quit your sport entirely: grueling training sessions, injuries that take months to heal, hard-nosed coaches, and tricky dynamics with teammates, to name a few. But when you face these situations with courage and wisdom, they build you up instead of breaking you down—and you can finish strong instead of bailing out.

THE CHARACTERISTICS OF RESILIENT ATHLETES

The first quality that sets resilient athletes apart is that they choose to stick with difficulty instead of giving up. They don't storm off the field or retreat in shame, vowing to never show their face in public again. Instead, they keep showing up, holding their heads high. They understand that setbacks are just part of life— nothing to be angry or embarrassed about. They take their cue from athletes like Tiger Woods and Bethany Hamilton, who are living proof that you can come back from just about any adversity.

If you can take a deep breath, mentally reset, and keep going when something goes wrong, you're already way ahead of the pack. And if you can stay hopeful and positive while doing it, you're practically guaranteed to emerge from the experience stronger. When you can say, "Man, that was grueling—but I wouldn't it change it for the world," you know you're on the right track.

Another, less-talked-about aspect of resilient athletes is that they don't try to handle everything alone. They aren't too proud to ask for advice from coaches, teammates, or sport clinicians. They understand that asking for help isn't a sign of weakness—it's a way to tap into their community's collective store of strength and knowledge, instead of relying on their own limited supply.

You can't build resilience by sitting alone in your room. The people around you, your team's culture, and your support systems all play a huge role in how well you bounce back from setbacks. Think about it: An athlete dealing with a serious injury will have a completely different experience depending on whether they have supportive teammates who keep checking in and including them versus teammates who move on and forget about them. An athlete who experienced a major blow to their confidence will recover more quickly if they have a coach who encourages them rather than benching them for the rest of the season, and a therapist who helps them work through the experience.

The good news is you have some level of control over these external factors. You can seek out mentors, build friendships with teammates, and develop the kind of support network that helps you be resilient. You *don't* have to be resilient on your own.

EMBRACING ADVERSITY

Duke women's basketball coach Kara Lawson teaches athletes to "handle hard better." In one of her impactful team speeches—recorded during a practice session and viewed online more than a million times—Coach Lawson challenged her players to think about difficulty and growth in a new way.

"We all wait in life for things to get easier," Lawson told her team. "It will never get easier. What happens is you handle hard better."

We tend to think of stress and pressure as temporary conditions we must "get through" so we can get back to being comfortable. But according to Lawson, stress and pressure are permanent features of any worthwhile pursuit. If you're doing something worthwhile, the challenges never stop coming. She concluded her speech, "Make yourself someone that handles hard well, and then whatever comes at you, you're going to be great."

When difficulty hits, your initial reaction sets the tone for everything that follows. If you ask yourself, "Why me?" or say, "This is going to ruin everything," you're missing an opportunity to build resilience. Instead, ask yourself, "What can this teach me?" or "OK, that happened—what can I do next?" Make a habit of focusing on your next move instead of getting mired in whatever setback you just experienced. Remember, the goal isn't to become someone who never struggles—it's to become someone who struggles *well*.

Emerson Midura, a lacrosse player at Harvard University and peer mentor at Kim's Athletes Better Together program, didn't make her high school varsity team the first year she tried out. This rejection crushed her self-confidence and sent her spiraling into doubts about her worth as both a player and a person. But that setback forced her to take an honest look at her game and identify what needed improvement: her mindset, stick skills, and physical strength. Instead of relying on external validation from coaches and teammates, she learned to build confidence from within—a skill that proved invaluable in competitive environments down the road. She spent the next year working on the gaps she'd identified, and when she tried out again, she made varsity. What started as devastation ultimately became the foundation for her success in high school and beyond.

DEALING WITH INJURIES

One of the biggest tests of your resilience as an athlete doesn't come from competition itself—often, it appears in the form of an injury. Unlike losing a game or missing a shot, where you can get right back out there and try again, an injury forces you into an entirely different kind of battle. It's a fight that happens largely in your head, away from the cheering crowds and bright lights, often in the sterile environment of a doctor's office or the quiet monotony of a physiotherapy clinic.

The summer before Kim's senior year of college, she was in the best shape of her life and excited to take on the responsibility of being co-captain of Harvard's women's hockey team. Then one weekend, she was hanging out with friends when she doubled over in excruciating pain. At the ER, doctors determined that her appendix had burst. The surgery for the ruptured appendix took over four hours. When doctors informed Kim that the recovery would take at least six weeks, she was devastated.

She still remembers the first walk she took after being cleared to get out of bed. Just one week before, she'd been benching her max in the gym. Now, she couldn't even take ten steps. *Oh my God*, Kim thought. *I'm supposed to be a leader for this team, and I won't be able to run for at least six weeks.*

What helped her through was a strong sense of purpose. She knew she needed to come back and be as strong as possible for her team when they reported in September. She had two months to get there and was determined. She made herself celebrate the small wins, like walking a little further each day. Even though she never quite regained the shape she was in before the emergency appendectomy, she found a new sense of resolve and gratitude for what she was able to do.

When you first get injured, especially if it's serious, the psychological impact can be just as devastating as the physical damage. You're suddenly faced with uncertainty about your future, questions about whether you'll ever be the same, and the crushing reality that your body—the very tool you've spent years perfecting—has betrayed you. The identity you've built around being an athlete gets shaken to its core. You might find yourself asking, "Who am I if I can't play?" and "Are my teammates really my friends, or do they just value me for my playing ability?"

The rehabilitation process itself can be a test of your character in ways that competition never could. In games, you get immediate feedback—you win or lose, you play well or poorly. But recovery is different. Progress is measured in millimeters and degrees of motion. Some days you feel stronger, and the next day you feel like you've taken two steps backward. The victories are smaller and harder to recognize. Pain may be your constant companion, and you may need to put as much effort into keeping a positive attitude as you do into the physical side of recovery.

The athletes who emerge strongest from injuries are those who learn to view the experience not simply as time stolen from their careers, but as an opportunity to develop parts of themselves they never knew existed. They use the forced break to study their sport more deeply, work on mental skills, strengthen other areas of their body, and keep building relationships with teammates.

If you're dealing with an injury right now, make a habit of identifying small wins every day. Maybe you did two more PT exercises than yesterday, or you spent thirty minutes visualizing your ice-skating routine even if you couldn't do it in real life. Maybe you studied up on your game by reading books or watching YouTube videos, or simply by sitting and watching your team practice.

Identifying small wins does two important things for you. First, it trains your brain to pay attention to the good stuff. As humans, we're naturally wired to focus on what goes wrong, so it takes real effort to start noticing the positive things happening around you or things you're doing well. When you make yourself look for the positives, you're training your brain to spot them. Eventually, this becomes a habit, and you'll start experiencing more positive emotions overall. That positive outlook becomes a buffer against the feelings of despair and frustration that can go along with an injury.

Second, focusing on small wins builds momentum. It helps you see that things *are* progressing instead of feeling like you're caught in an infinite loop of waking up every morning not being able to do the things you're used to doing. Noticing these incremental improvements gives you a motivational boost and provides additional defense against falling into despair. In the words of NFL player Emmett Smith, "Winning is something that builds physically and mentally every day that you train and every night that you dream." This is true both during the times when you're at your physical peak *and* when you're putting in the hard work of recovering from an injury.

⌣

Resilience doesn't mean becoming invincible or never struggling. It means becoming a person who struggles well, bounces back stronger, and refuses to see their setbacks as insurmountable. Overcoming real challenges builds confidence, recovering from injuries forces you to develop the mental side of your game, and showing up for practice after a crushing defeat gives your teammates a chance to show their support. Eventually, you just might find that you no longer fear the hard stuff, having realized that you can handle way more than you thought you could.

SKILL TO TRY: RESILIENCE INVENTORY

Remembering times when you were resilient in the past can boost your confidence and equip you to be more resilient in the future.

Once a week, set aside ten minutes to consciously recall a time you demonstrated resilience in your sport or life, even if the outcome wasn't what you hoped for.

As you're reflecting on this memory, ask yourself what traits helped you be victorious. What did you take from those moments, and what did you learn? How are you a better person or athlete from having worked through that moment?

Write down your answers. Over time, you'll build a personal record of resilience you can turn to whenever you need inspiration.

CHAPTER 9
optimizing mindset

Becca was a college golfer who'd been a highly ranked recruit coming out of high school. At their first session, Becca told Jonathan that if she didn't shoot par on most holes and didn't achieve a birdie on every par 3, she saw her round as a failure. "I'll say to myself, I'm such an idiot *and* I'm going to lose, I don't even know why I showed up today!"

After even one bad hole, Becca would start to spiral. Then she'd overcorrect on the next hole: If she'd overshot the green, she'd be too timid and leave it short. If she'd sliced the ball right, she'd aim too far left. Before tournaments, Becca would toss and turn all night and wake up with a queasy stomach. Becca believed that she only had worth if she was playing well, and when that didn't happen, she would talk about how much of a burden she was on her teammates.

Jonathan worked with Becca to examine her self-talk and encouraged her to notice and redirect "all-or-nothing" negative thoughts. She learned to speak to herself in a positive and encouraging way, focusing on what she was doing right. Slowly, Becca began to manage her blowups on the golf course, and her play improved soon after.

"I never realized that the words I said inside my head had any effect on my physical performance," Becca told Jonathan. "But the

connection is so strong. Now, I'm always careful about what I'm tell-ing myself when I think nobody can hear me. Those words have a direct link to how I play."

———

Your mindset is the lens through which you view every situa-tion—the set of beliefs and attitudes that determine whether you interpret neutral events as threats or opportunities. Mind-set is one of the few aspects of sport that is entirely within your control. You can't control if your opponent is having the game of their life. You can't control if it starts pouring rain. You can't control if the crowd is hostile or the referee makes a dicey call. But you *can* choose how you respond to these situations.

Think about two athletes facing the exact same situation—maybe they're both down by two points with a minute left on the clock. One athlete thinks, *This is it, we're going to lose; I always choke in these moments.* The other athlete thinks, *We still have an entire minute to turn things around.* Same situation, completely different interpretation. Which athlete do you think has a better chance of leading their team to victory?

Owning your attitude is extremely liberating. As American in-dustrialist Henry Ford put it, "Whether you think you can or think you can't, you're right." In other words, your mind has already de-cided the range of possible outcomes before your body even gets the chance to try. If you've made your mind up that it's not worth trying, your body will never show you what it's truly capable of.

In the early 1950s, the four-minute mile stood like an invis-ible wall that no runner could break through. People had come tantalizingly close, clocking times of 4:01 and 4:02, but that final barrier still stood. Medical experts even warned that attempting to break the four-minute mark would cause a runner's heart to explode. Everyone seemed to accept this as an established fact—except for a British runner named Roger Bannister.

A neurologist by training, Bannister approached the challenge like a scientist. He used interval training, pacing by his teammates, and paying attention to minute details like rubbing graphite on his racing spikes so they wouldn't pick up too much cinder ash from the track. Most importantly, however, he refused to accept the "fact" that a four-minute mile was impossible.

On a cold, windy day at Oxford's Iffley Road track, Bannister lined up for what would become one of the most famous races in history. He ran a mile in 3:59—and the crowd went wild.

But here's where the story gets really interesting. Just forty-six days later, another runner broke Bannister's record. Then another. And another. Today, more than 2,000 runners have broken the four-minute mile—a feat that was "impossible" until one person refused to believe the limitation was real. What changed wasn't human physiology—it was mindset. As soon as Bannister proved it could be done, the mental barrier crumbled for everyone else, a phenomenon now commonly referred to as the "Bannister Effect."

ACTING "AS IF"

Roger Bannister acted "as if" he was capable of beating the four-minute mile—and he proved himself right. The all-time winningest Ivy League basketball coach, Kathy Delaney-Smith, taught the same attitude to her players. She would say things like, "If you're at the end of a game and your legs are feeling tired, act as if you have endless energy. If you start worrying that someone is going to beat you in a one-on-one, act as if you *know* you're going to stop them."

Kim's time at Harvard University overlapped with Delaney-Smith's, and this "act as if" mentality permeated her hockey team as well. When Coach Katey Stone would put them through a grueling practice, her teammates would tell each other, "Act as if you love this drill." The effect was extraordinary. Instead of just enduring the drill and waiting for practice to be over, Kim and her teammates found themselves engaging with the process wholeheartedly, and with the humor necessary to make it actually fun. When you act "as if" you love something challenging, your brain starts hunting for reasons why this might be true—and your pretend enjoyment can turn to genuine appreciation.

When you're deep in a grueling training cycle, facing intense pressure from coaches, teammates, and yourself, it's easy to lose sight of a fundamental truth: you chose this. Nobody forced you to pick up that stick, lace up those cleats, or step onto that court. You're here because at some point, you fell in love with this sport.

But somewhere along the way, we tend to forget that crucial fact. What started as "Wow, I get to play!" turns into "Oh no, I have to perform." Without even realizing it, your mindset drifts from gratitude and excitement to fear and dread.

Kim's favorite fitness instructor and sports reporter, Jess Sims, teaches the motto, "You don't have to, you *get* to." When Sims leads her Peloton clients through brutal workouts, she doesn't let them suffer through it. Instead, she reminds them that having a healthy body capable of exercise is a gift and that choosing to do hard things is a sign of self-respect. By embracing this positive mindset, Sims and her #GetToCrew flip the script on exhausting workouts by seeing them as a privilege, not a punishment.

When you're feeling stressed about an upcoming game or practice, remind yourself of how excited and proud you felt when you earned a spot on this team in the first place. Remember how lucky you are that you have the free time in which to exercise and play sports when many people around the world have no choice but to spend every waking moment working. Think about the gifts that physical fitness has brought to your life—not just a strong body, but friendships, opportunities, and wisdom. You don't *have* to do this—you *get* to.

STRATEGIC SELF-TALK

One of the most powerful tools you can use to optimize your mindset is something you already do thousands of times a day: talking to yourself. You're already the first person you talk to when you wake up in the morning, the last person you talk to before you go to sleep, and the one person with whom you're guaranteed to maintain an ongoing dialogue with throughout the day. Why not make this round-the-clock conversation a good one?

Elite athletes across every sport have mastered the art of strategic self-talk. As American surfer Laird Hamilton once said, "Make sure your worst enemy doesn't live between your own two ears." Tennis legend Pete Sampras was known for his ability to stay calm and collected even when matches weren't going his way. He'd mentally repeat phrases like "everything is okay" to calm his nerves, then redirect his attention with phrases like "let go of that last point and focus on the next point." When he needed to change his physical approach, he'd use action-oriented cues like "get aggressive with your feet." This systematic and intentional approach to self-talk helped him maintain confidence and perform under pressure throughout his legendary career.

Simone Biles, the most decorated gymnast in U.S. history, has a consistent ritual: before stepping onto the mat, she takes a deep breath and mentally repeats a single word like "confidence" or a short phrase like "you got this." When NBA player LeBron James needs to get focused and motivated, he talks about himself in the third person, as if he's observing from the outside: "LeBron needs to be more aggressive" or "LeBron has to take over this game." This technique, known as self-distancing, helps create psychological space between the person and the pressure. By referring to himself in the third person, James can evaluate situations more objectively and give himself direction without the emotional weight that comes with first-person criticism or pressure.

Self-talk is the set of emotional instructions your mind and body follow. If that voice in your head is saying you're not good enough, your performance on the field or in the gym will reflect that belief. If it tells you that a certain event was a disaster, you'll feel that fear or embarrassment in your body and mind. But if your self-talk is centered on reassuring you and keeping you focused on the present moment, your mind and body will follow those instructions, too.

There are four types of self-talk:

- **Spontaneous self-talk** is the unfiltered commentary that pops into your head—your brain's immediate reaction to whatever's happening around you or within you. This is the voice that says, "I can't believe I did that!" when you miss an easy shot, or "Yes!" when you make a perfect play. Spontaneous self-talk can feel very automatic and hard to control—but with practice, you can learn to redirect it.

- **Goal-directed self-talk** is more intentional and purposeful, helping you focus on a given task and execute it well. This type of self-talk often consists of giving yourself actionable instructions—things like "take a breath" or "swing through the ball."

One great thing about goal-directed self-talk is that it helps you stay present. When you anchor yourself to a thought like "smooth follow-through," you're not dwelling on that mistake you made a few minutes ago, or worrying about the score. Instead, you're guiding your mind to attend to the task that's right in front of you, right now.

- **Positive self-talk** means being your own biggest fan, building your self-efficacy with thoughts like "I got this" or "nice pass." When you consistently notice and celebrate your good plays, you build a reservoir of confidence you can draw on when the going gets tough. This isn't about putting on a cheerful veneer or suppressing negative emotions—it's about increasing your capacity to notice the positive in a sincere and genuine way.

- **Motivational self-talk** means tapping into your inner warrior—the part of you that can inspire you to keep pushing even when your whole body hurts, the situation seems hopeless, and you want to give up. This kind of self-talk can help you rise above overwhelm and exhaustion and achieve things you didn't know were possible. Statements like "keep working" or "go harder" can help you dig deep and access that inner reservoir of energy and courage that lives within each one of us. The key is to find words or phrases that connect to your values and ignite your competitive spirit.

Learning to speak to yourself in a positive way may sound like fluff, but sport psychology research has consistently demonstrated that athletes who train their internal dialogue see measurable improvements in both their mental health and their athletic performance. A 2020 study by Park, Lim, and Kim on Korean shooters in the *Journal of Sports Science & Medicine* found that athletes who practiced positive self-talk techniques didn't just perform better—they enjoyed their sport more and felt more intrinsically motivated to keep working at it. Other research has linked self-talk training to decreased anxiety and improved confidence, self-efficacy, and performance. When you learn how to manage your internal dialogue, your scores improve, your consistency increases, and your ability to perform under pressure gets stronger. The voice in your head isn't just commenting on your athletic performance—it's actively shaping it.

Just as important as cultivating positive self-talk is eliminating negative self-talk—that voice in your head scolding you for missing your shot or failing to meet your time. Your brain doesn't really know the difference between facts and opinions—so if you're always telling yourself "I suck," your brain is eventually going to start believing it. Although negative self-talk might feel like self-discipline or having high standards, over time it will erode your self-confidence, undermine your performance, and make you more likely to make mistakes.

The first step in training your self-talk is awareness. Start paying attention to your internal commentary, especially during stressful moments. What do you say to yourself after a bad play? How do you talk to yourself when you're nervous before a big game? How do these things affect your performance?

During your next practice, try using a simple five-point scale to keep track of your self-talk. Start by giving yourself a baseline score of three—completely neutral self-talk. As you move through different drills and situations, pay attention to your self-talk and assess whether your score has gone up or down. A score of one means your inner voice is being very negative, while a five means it's being consistently positive and supportive. How does your score fluctuate throughout the practice? Is it easier for you to practice positive self-talk in some situations than others? Where is negative self-talk most likely to pop up?

This thermometer approach helps you become aware of patterns you might not have noticed before. You might realize that your self-talk tanks during individual skill work when you feel like everyone's watching, but stays positive during scrimmages when you're focused on the team. Or maybe you notice that your inner critic gets louder toward the end of practice when you're tired and sore, or when the coach is running a drill you hate. These observations let you know exactly when and where you need to be most intentional about managing your self-talk.

Once you've established a baseline of awareness about your self-talk patterns, you can start actively interrupting negative thoughts before they spiral out of control. One of the most effective techniques for this is called "thought stopping." When you catch yourself having a thought like "I can never beat this opponent" or "I'm just going to get injured again," immediately visualize a bright red stop sign or a large X. You can also think or speak the word "STOP" while visualizing this image. The more quickly and clearly you call up this image and think this word, the more effectively it breaks the negative thought pattern.

SELF-TALK TROUBLESHOOTING

Just like learning to shoot a perfect free throw or nail a complex gymnastics routine, mastering the art of positive self-talk takes practice. When you start changing your internal dialogue, it's going to feel a little awkward or unnatural at first. You might find yourself thinking, *Who is this stranger who's taken up residence inside my head?* or *Aren't I just lying to myself?* This discomfort is normal. After all, you're rewiring years of entrenched habits, and making major changes to the version of "you" with whom you're most familiar. Trust that the more often you practice using positive, motivational, and goal-directed statements with yourself, the more these statements will start to feel like second nature.

If positive self-talk feels too hard at first, start with motivational or instructional self-talk. Tell yourself something about the technique you're focusing on, like "pull," "drive," "hips through," or anything related to the mechanics of your sport. Once you gain some familiarity with these instructional statements, try adding some positive and encouraging statements and see how it feels. If you can tolerate it, keep going! Soon, positive self-talk will start to feel natural and automatic. Most importantly, you will start to *believe* the positive statements you're making about yourself.

If you're not sure if your self-talk is healthy or not, ask yourself if you would say the same thing, in the same tone, to a friend or teammate. If the answer is yes, you're on the right track. On the other hand, if you feel like it would be rude or cruel to say this to a teammate, you should absolutely never say it to yourself. Even if you think of yourself as a person who can "take the heat," contemptuous or harsh self-talk is always going to be less effective than positive self-talk at bringing out your peak performance.

SELF-TALK GOES BEYOND WORDS

Self-talk isn't just about the voice in your head—your body is part of the conversation, too. The way you carry yourself, your facial expressions, and your physical reactions all send powerful messages to your brain, your teammates, and your opponents.

Think about the difference between two players after they make a mistake. One drops their shoulders, hangs their head, and trudges back into position with a look of defeat. The other stands tall, takes a deep breath, and claps their hands together before getting ready for the next play. Both players made the same error, but their bodies are telling completely different stories about what that mistake means and what happens next.

Your brain takes cues from your body language just as much as your thoughts. When you slouch and look defeated, you're not just showing others that you're discouraged—you're actually making yourself *feel* more discouraged. Conversely, when you maintain strong posture and confident gestures, you're sending a signal to your nervous system that you're still in control and ready to compete. Just think of the way that WNBA All-Star Kelsey Plum purposefully smiles at the free throw line, a trick she learned from her father as a kid to project a sense of calm and ease to everyone around her and to herself.

Positive body language becomes especially powerful in team sports, where your physical presence can either lift up or bring down the energy of the people around you. Teammates are keenly aware of how you handle adversity. Are you the player who stays composed and ready, or the one whose body language communicates defeat? Physical confidence is contagious. It tells everyone the game isn't over and there's still work to be done. When you can communicate this kind of resilience on a consistent basis, you naturally become a leader for the people around you.

The best part about body language is that it's completely under your control, even when your emotions aren't. You might feel frustrated, scared, or nervous on the inside, but you can still choose to stand tall, make eye contact, and send the message that you're ready for whatever's coming next. This creates a positive feedback loop that makes you stronger inside and out. How you hold your body affects your mindset—a form of wordless self-talk that's just as effective as the verbal kind.

⌒

Just as Roger Bannister proved that breaking the four-minute mile was possible by refusing to accept conventional limits and working thoughtfully to overcome them, you have the power to shatter your own invisible barriers with the way you think and talk to yourself. When you master your self-talk, choose empowering body language, and learn to act "as if" you're already the athlete you want to become, you're removing self-imposed obstacles and stepping into your full potential.

SKILL TO TRY:
RECOGNIZE AND REPLACE

The first step of training your self-talk is developing your ability to **recognize** what you're saying and how it impacts your play.

If you find that your self-talk does not help or has a negative impact, you must **replace** it with positive or goal-directed self-talk.

In practice, it could look like this: A hockey player on the boards with the puck breaking out of the zone could find himself making a self-talk statement of "don't mess up" or "don't throw it away" when a more positive or goal-oriented way of talking to himself during this situation would be to say, "I got this" or "head up."

INSTEAD OF THIS ... TRY THIS!

Negative Self-Talk	Positive Self-Talk
"I can't do this."	"I will improve."
"Don't screw up."	"I got this."
"I can't believe I did that."	"Focus on the next play."
"I suck."	"I can bounce back."

mistakes and perfectionism

Kim once worked with a Division I hockey team that had started the season strong by winning their first six games against teams ranked higher than them. Then they lost two games in a row to teams they should have beaten easily.

When Kim first met with the team, she could feel the tension and confusion in the room. "We don't understand what's happening," the captain told her. "We were at 6-0 and now it feels like we're in free fall."

After some questioning, it became apparent that those six big wins had created a ton of pressure. Players now expected themselves to win every game—and to make it look easy. The elation they felt at the beginning of the season had turned to stress, as they went into each game dreading the end of their winning streak. As one player explained, "We went from playing like we had nothing to lose to playing like we had everything to lose."

The fear of failure meant they'd stopped taking risks and stopped having fun. The more they thought about their next move, the harder it was to get into a flow state. It was clear that if things went on like this, the team was going to get burned out.

Once the team realized that perfectionism was strangling their performance, everything changed. With Kim's help, they developed new team norms, like celebrating effort regardless of outcome, and encouraging healthy risk-taking. "We'd gotten so focused on being perfect we couldn't actually play," the team captain reflected later. "Shifting our focus to the process saved us from a really bad downward spiral."

One of the toughest situations we face in sports is how to recover after making a mistake. No matter how hard you prepare, mistakes are still going to happen—and if you get hung up on them, it will stop you from picking yourself up and finishing strong. From Tom Brady dropping a pass in the Super Bowl to Shaun White crashing during his first run on the snowboarding half-pipe at the Sochi Olympics, mistakes are ubiquitous in the world of sports, and nobody is exempt from making them—even the GOATS among us.

Understanding how to handle mistakes gets even harder when there's perfectionism involved. In her book *How to Be Enough*, Boston University clinical psychologist Ellen Hendriksen explains, "Perfectionism isn't about striving to be perfect. It's about never feeling good enough." If you've wondered why the perfectionist on your team never seems to be satisfied, even after a spectacular performance, that's why. Perfectionism convinces us that mistakes aren't just errors, but proof that we are bad, unacceptable, and maybe even unlovable—when none of those things are true.

Perfectionism can come from a number of sources: coaches whose eyes go dim when your performance is anything less than exceptional, parents who raised you to bring home straight A's, or social media reels showing only perfect performances while editing out all the fumbles and wobbles along the way.

Wanting to be great at your sport is normal and healthy. Who *doesn't* want to feel the thrill of executing a skill perfectly and the satisfaction that comes from making a major contribution to your team? Perfectionism, however, takes these desires to an extreme that drains the joy out of sports, replacing it with a rigid obsessiveness or even fear. When you're a perfectionist, your mentality becomes fixated on fulfilling one sometimes arbitrary measure of success while ignoring all the other factors that make life and sports meaningful.

Up until her mid-twenties, Kim was a textbook perfectionist both on and off the ice. When her world and emotions felt chaotic, she would color-coordinate her underwear drawer to regain a sense of control. She would make herself cut certain things from her diet, stay at the library until a certain time, or train for a marathon in six weeks.

As a hockey player at Harvard, Kim had a very tough time rebounding from mistakes. If she gave up the puck in the defensive zone, she felt so much shame and embarrassment that when she got off the ice, she'd shrink on the bench, wanting to disappear. She'd punish herself with negative thoughts, and used hunched-over body language to make sure her teammates knew that *she* knew how badly she'd screwed up. In fact, one of the reasons Kim became a sport clinician was to make sure that other young athletes don't experience the depth of self-imposed suffering that she did.

In Kim's Senior year at Harvard, a teammate came into her dorm room while her color-coordinated underwear drawer was open. She took one look and said, "How long does it take you to *do* this?" Kim thought for a moment and realized she had no idea;

it was just something she'd always done. Her teammate huffed. "What a waste of time!" she said. "You have a whole life to live— why are you stressing about getting your underwear perfect?"

This honest reaction from her teammate was a turning point in Kim's life. She realized how much time and energy she'd been pouring into things that didn't really matter in the hopes that being more perfect would make her feel safe.

The journalist and social activist Gloria Steinem once wrote, "Perfectionism is internalized oppression." In other words, the function of perfectionism isn't to lift us up, but to keep us trapped. How? By constantly moving the goalpost, promising a sense of safety and fulfillment that's always just out of reach. If you've ever achieved a longed-for goal, only to immediately start feeling sad, anxious, and self-critical again, you know that the rewards of perfectionism are more often a mirage.

Despite its high costs, there can be a few advantages to perfectionism. Athletes who have perfectionistic tendencies typically have great attention to detail, are highly motivated, and relentlessly pursue their goals. But when you give perfectionism free rein without setting appropriate boundaries, it leads to high stress, anxiety, depression, and burnout. Ultimately, perfectionism can give you a fear of failure that gets in the way of your success—which defeats the whole point!

PERFECTIONISM AND TEAMWORK

Perfectionism isn't just an individual issue—it can affect entire teams. During the 2022–2023 regular season, the Boston Bruins were killing it. They not only ended with a 65-12-5 record, giving them the most wins and points in an NHL season, but they also had one of the best goal differentials ever—a whopping +128. Their record at the Boston Garden was unmatched, winning thirty-four contests and only dropping four games at home with three ties. The Bruins entered the postseason on top of the world, with aspirations of bringing home the Stanley Cup more than ten years after winning it in 2011.

Those hopes were shattered in their first-round matchup with the Florida Panthers, the eighth seed in their conference. After taking a 3-1 lead in the best-of-seven series, the Bruins lost in Game 7 and left the playoffs shellshocked and filled with regret. Just like the Division I hockey team Kim worked with, their earlier winning streak had established high expectations and incredible pressure to never make mistakes. As a Boston. com article written by Conor Ryan put it, "[The] 2022–23 Bruins' season was toppled by days of uncharacteristic missteps, second-guesses and logic-defying gaffes—all doled out by their greatest foe, themselves."

While there's nothing wrong with wanting to play your best, it's important for both individuals *and* teams to strive for consistent, daily excellence instead of random streaks of perfection. This can be tough when you grew up marveling at "Top Ten" plays on ESPN and scrolling through viral sport reels on your favorite social media platforms. This tsunami of media can create the illusion that "perfect plays" are happening all the time, when the reality is that these beautiful moments are incredibly rare.

The truth is, most games and competitions aren't won by dazzling plays, but by minimizing errors, honing fundamentals, and capitalizing on key moments. More games are won without a flashy play than with one. Understanding this fact will help you approach competition with the right mindset and priorities.

Think about the games you've watched where one team dominated the highlight reels but lost on the scoreboard. The flashy team might have been more exciting to watch, but they probably also fumbled some plays at crucial moments. Meanwhile, the winning team executed the basics flawlessly—they protected the ball, communicated on defense, and made good passes every time. The team that capitalizes on most of their easy opportunities will usually beat the team that makes a few unbelievable plays but struggles with fundamentals, and the athlete who rarely makes an unforced error will ultimately outperform the one who astounds people with their brilliance but makes sloppy mistakes or gets paralyzed by perfectionism.

THE COGNITIVE TRIANGLE

The Cognitive Triangle is a tool developed by the psychiatrist Aaron Beck—also known as the founder of Cognitive Behavioral Therapy—in the 1960s. It illustrates the ways our thoughts, behaviors, and emotions feed into one another, creating either a virtuous cycle or a vicious one. Although we may believe that a certain event or situation *causes* us to feel and act in a certain way, the Cognitive Triangle shows that it is in fact our *perception* of the situation that determines our actions.

For example, let's say you're a soccer player who's just been taken off the field by your coach. All you know is you've been pulled out of the game—you don't know why. What happens next depends entirely on how your mind interprets what just occurred. If you think you got pulled out because you made a mistake, you'll feel difficult emotions like shame or frustration, and you might respond by withdrawing or lashing out. If, on the other hand, you think the coach pulled you out to give a chance to a different player who hasn't had much playing time, you might feel a sense of appreciation for the coach's fairness, and you might cheer on your teammates happily during your time on the bench.

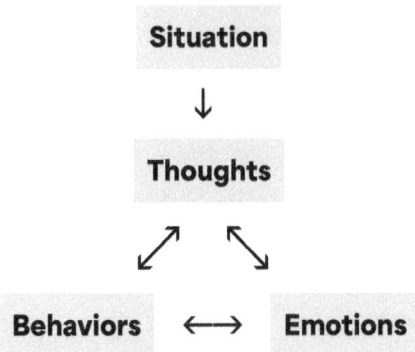

Any athlete who's gone down a doom spiral after making a mistake knows how quickly things can unravel. Your emotions tank, your thoughts start looping, and you find yourself saying and doing things you later regret. Later on, when you can look back on the situation objectively, you realize this spiral was completely unnecessary—but by then, it's too late.

The key to replacing a vicious cycle with a virtuous one is to understand that even though you can't directly control how you feel, you can use the other two points on the cognitive triangle to bring yourself back to a positive frame of mind. You do this by changing the way you *think* about the situation and making wise decisions about how to *act* in response to it. When you do these two things, you naturally start to *feel* better.

For example, our athlete who feels angry and upset about being taken out of the game by her coach may not be able to change how she feels about it in that exact moment, but she does have the power to immediately challenge her thinking about the situation and her actions. Her first action could be to label what she's feeling by saying to herself, "I'm feeling angry," and then telling herself, "I'm having the thought that my coach hates me," as a way to separate the thought from herself. Next, she could take a deep breath to reduce her physical arousal. All of these techniques protect her from going into a negative spiral and improve the odds that she'll be ready to perform her best when the coach puts her back on the field.

USING CUE STATEMENTS

One powerful tool you can use to bounce back from mistakes is a **cue statement**: a word or phrase you say to yourself to quickly move past a setback and refocus your mind on the present. Cue statements should be brief, feel natural to you, and be positive or neutral rather than negative: for example, "reset," "next play," "you got this," or "flush it."

Grace Murphy, captain of the Stonehill College women's lacrosse team and peer mentor at Kim's Athletes Better Together program, discovered how powerful cue statements can be for resetting after mistakes. She shared with Kim that dropping the ball during a crucial man-up situation used to send her into a spiral of anger and self-criticism. "My first thought would be to get frustrated and annoyed at myself for making a mistake like that on such an important possession," she recalled. But Grace realized that her negative reaction was making things worse. The anger and self-blame would lead to another mistake, like committing an unnecessary foul that set her team back even further.

To break this pattern, she developed a simple but effective cue statement: "next play." This two-word phrase became her mental reset button, immediately redirecting her focus from what went wrong to what she could do right in the next moment. The result wasn't just better performance—it was a healthier relationship with herself on the field.

QUICK RESETS

Every athlete needs a handful of mental reset tools in their tool-kit—things you can reach for quickly without needing to think too hard. Here are a few that we use with athletes in our practice every day:

FOCUS ON THE CONTROLLABLES

You can't always control if you make a mistake in a game, but you can control how you respond to it. In fact, you can sum up this simple truth in a simple equation created by author and motivational speaker Jack Canfield: **Event + Response = Outcome**. Notice that in this equation the only thing you can control is your response, and it is how you respond that will help dictate the outcome.

The next time you make a mistake, immediately ask yourself the question, "What can I still control?" Maybe that's your body language. Maybe that's the words you say or refrain from saying. Maybe that's how hard you lean into the next play. The more you practice this skill, the more you'll realize you can still control your response, even when you've just slipped up.

FOCUS ON SOMETHING YOU'RE GOOD AT

If you've recently made a mistake that's shaken your confidence deeply—like crashing during a ski jump—try shifting your focus to any activity at which you're highly competent. For example, if you know how to juggle, try juggling for a few minutes; if you know how to pop a handstand or do a perfect cartwheel, do that. This will help you shake off the mistake and restore your confidence that you *do* know how to execute physical tasks.

MAKE A RITUAL ADJUSTMENT

Sometimes, a quick ritual involving your gear or clothing can help you signal to yourself that you're resetting after a mistake. For example, you could adjust your helmet, retie your shoes, wipe the sweat off your forehead with a towel, or simply shake your hands as if they're wet and you're flicking the water away. This kind of clear physical gesture can help you meet the next moment as a fresh start, not a continuation of the mistake.

REFLECTING ON MISTAKES

In addition to learning to bounce back from mistakes in the moment, it is also important to know how to effectively reflect on mistakes after the game or competition. This doesn't mean beating yourself up for mistakes, but analyzing them thoughtfully and objectively so you can glean useful data from them. Try to look at your mistakes like a scientist—really drain out the emotions and focus only on the facts. What happened? Why did it happen? What could you have done differently? What did you learn?

In his book *The Creative Act*, influential music producer and co-founder of Def Jam Recordings Rick Rubin wrote, "Failure is the information you need to get where you're going." Without occasional mistakes or failures, you'd never get the insight or feedback you need to improve and push further. In fact, if you did everything "perfectly" every time, that's probably a sign that you're not taking enough risks or reaching for hard enough goals.

To process mistakes after a game or competition, you can try journaling, reviewing film of the game or performance, or talking with teammates and coaches to get more feedback about what went wrong and what to do differently the next time. It is critical to process mistakes in a non-judgmental way and completely disconnect the mistake from your own self-worth as a person. Never let your mistakes define you.

—

Let us be honest with you: bouncing back from mistakes takes work and is a hard skill to master. And although society commonly portrays success and failure as opposite experiences, this could not be further from the truth. There is no success without failure. In fact, success almost never comes from playing it safe. The risks you take and the mistakes you make build you into a better athlete, and it's impossible to become truly elite without them.

SKILL TO TRY:
WEEK/MONTH/YEAR REFLECTION

If after reflecting on your mistake post-game or competition you still feel stuck, you can try asking yourself, "Will I remember this mistake in a week? A month? A year?" If not, give yourself permission to drop it. On the other hand, if you identify a genuine lesson from the mistake—like "I need to communicate better on defense" or "I start to rush when I'm tired"—bring that insight to your next practice and actively work on it.

Head to www.mentalitywins.com/resources for a "Rule of 5 Worksheet," a take on author James Altucher's 5x5 Rule of Life, where you can list common stressors and report whether you think they'll bother you in five seconds, five minutes, five days, five weeks, five months, or five years.

CHAPTER 11
grit and self-mastery

Ford was a forty-year-old ultramarathon runner with a frustrating pattern: he'd spend months training, feel invincible for the first seventy miles of a hundred-mile race, then hit a wall and drop out with thirty miles left to go.

"I feel so ashamed," he told Jonathan. "I know my body can handle it, but the voice in my head starts telling me it's impossible, and once that starts happening I just can't follow through."

Jonathan worked with Ford to create what they called his "grit protocol"—a three-part plan focusing on micro-goals, adversity rehearsal, and post-run debriefs where he would notice and celebrate his ability to overcome "quiet quit" moments. Instead of thinking, Holy crap, I need to run a hundred miles, *he learned to think,* I just need to make it to the next aid station.

Jonathan and Ford spent sessions visualizing the exact moments when Ford most wanted to quit—usually when he saw a cue in his environment that reminded him of how many miles he still had to run to reach the finish line—and practiced the self-mastery techniques that would get him through.

At his next race, Ford was feeling good until mile seventy-two, when he hit what ultrarunners call "the wall"—massive elevation gain combined with muscle soreness that made every step feel like torture. But this time was different. Instead of thinking, I still have twenty-eight miles to go, *Ford focused on cresting the next hill. When thoughts of quitting crept in, he dedicated each step to two close friends who had recently passed away.*

"I literally asked them for help," *Ford said later.* "And I swear I could feel them carrying me up those mountains." *He crossed the finish line for the first time in his racing career, tears streaming down his face.*

———

Psychologist Angela Duckworth defines grit like this: "Grit is about having what some researchers call an 'ultimate concern'—a goal you care about so much that it organizes and gives meaning to almost everything you do. Grit is holding steadfast to that goal. Even when you fall down. Even when you screw up. Even when progress toward that goal is halting or slow."

After years of studying what predicts success among all types of people, Duckworth found that it wasn't talent or intelligence, but grittiness that set extremely successful individuals apart. In fact, she found that natural talent can sometimes work *against* long-term success if people coast on their gifts instead of developing self-discipline and a strong work ethic.

Being a gritty athlete means having a true love of your sport combined with relentless practice to continue honing your skills. If you feel passionate about your sport but don't demonstrate perseverance, you may love what you do but never push yourself hard enough to unlock your full potential. Conversely, if you're good at persevering but don't really love your sport, that lack of day-to-day enjoyment will quickly lead to burnout, no matter how masterful you become. The key to longevity and success as an athlete is to cultivate both passion *and* perseverance.

NBA player Steph Curry is an athlete who exemplifies true grit. He has persisted through all types of adversity, including being one of the smaller players throughout his career, not getting top NCAA scholarship offers, and having repeated ankle injuries. He says, "We have to have the mentality that we have to work for everything we're going to get." This attitude—that his success comes from perseverance and hard work, not from raw talent alone—is what sets Curry apart from his competitors.

Are you gritty? One way to know is to think about what you do when things don't come easy. Do you dig deeper and find the resolve you need to keep fighting, or do you tell yourself it's a hopeless case? Do you keep trying even when you're the "worst" player in the competition and it seems like you'll never catch up to everyone else? Do you feel so passionate about your sport that you can't imagine living without it, even if you never win prizes or accolades?

If you've been playing sports for a long time, you've probably shown way more moments of grit than you've given yourself credit for: That time you showed up for the playoff game even though you were fighting off an ear infection. The winter you went for a run every day, even when the temperature plunged to twenty below. The time you showed up for a competition and gave it your all even when you were the least likely to win. The good news is, you can keep growing your grit throughout your athletic career. Just as the grit in a river carves a stunning canyon, the grit you demonstrate day after day carves out the best possible version of yourself.

EMBRACING A GROWTH MINDSET

Stanford psychologist Carol Dweck coined the term "growth mindset" to describe the belief that you can develop your abilities through dedication and hard work. When you have a growth mindset, you believe that no matter how much of a beginner you are, you can improve by putting in the effort and learning from your mistakes. In contrast, a "fixed mindset" is the belief that your abilities are more or less set in stone, and there's no point in trying to move past your limitations.

A fixed mindset tells you, *You've never been a fast skater, your real talent is stickhandling, so don't even bother working on speed.* A growth mindset says, *You're not as fast as you could be, but that's because you've put most of your energy into stickhandling. With some hard work, you can become an explosive skater, too.*

Even though it seems clear that a growth mindset is preferable to a fixed one, we often steer clear of working on our weaker skills just because we don't like to see ourselves fail. We'd rather practice things we're already good at because it feels safe—even if bolstering our weaknesses will make us better players overall.

Athletes who embrace a growth mindset don't see any specific weakness as a permanent condition. Instead, they see that weakness as territory they're traveling through on their way to something better. They say, "Man, I used to be the *worst* at that thing, but when I started spending thirty minutes a day on it, it got better and better. Now I can barely remember why I struggled so much." As Dweck writes in *Mindset: The New Psychology of Success,* "Picture your brain forming new connections as you meet the challenge and learn." When you're standing still, those new connections aren't forming. It's only by trying hard, pushing yourself, and giving yourself the *opportunity* to show grit that you will experience real growth.

GROWING YOUR GRIT

Real grit starts with genuine love for your sport—not just basking in the big wins and moments of glory, but relishing the daily grind. You have to love the ache in your muscles, the sweaty clothes in your laundry bin, the silly nicknames your teammates call you, and how you're so hungry after practice you could devour an entire lasagna. Pay attention to these sparks and hold on to them, especially when things get tough—that passion is what helps you persevere.

Gritty people develop a taste for what's known as "Type 2 fun." This phrase was coined by Dr. Rainier Newberry, a geologist and mountaineer at the University of Alaska, after he noticed that his best memories of mountaineering often came from the most miserable experiences. Slogging through a cold, wet day with your buddies gives you something to laugh and reminisce about when you're sitting by a warm fire, whereas an easy, uneventful day doesn't give us the same level of bonding or positive emotions.

The hardest parts of sports—driving cross-country on a bus to go to games, waking up at 4 a.m. to practice, enduring a brutal defeat against a rival and getting bag skated afterwards—can all be thought of as Type 2 fun. When you get together with your teammates for a postseason celebration, you probably spend a little time reminiscing about the perfect plays—but even *more* time talking about the incident when you all got food poisoning at the Holiday Inn the night before that big playoff game. Growing your grit means learning to love the parts of sport that are only fun once they're safely in the rearview mirror.

Grit also means showing up with intention. Anyone can go through the motions and call it practice, but gritty athletes make every minute count. Before you start, know exactly what you're trying to improve. During practice, give it everything you've got—not just physically, but mentally, too. Let yourself get sweaty, hoarse, and out of breath (but stop short of injuring yourself!). Afterward, let yourself be completely exhausted. The only way you'll ever discover the true size of your gas tank is to occasionally run it dry.

Finally, grit means refusing to blame others for your circumstances and choosing to make the most of whatever situation you find yourself in. Gritty athletes rarely say, "That was unfair" or "I couldn't help it." Instead, they look within and constantly ask themselves how they can be steering their ship in the direction they want to go. After all, blaming others or the world at large will rarely improve your situation—but working harder will.

Greg Harden was a mental health and performance coach who worked with high-achieving athletes like Tom Brady and Michael Phelps. In his book *Stay Sane in an Insane World: How to Control the Controllables and Thrive*, he wrote, "The best way to completely lose your steam is to see your own circumstances and your own state of mind as something outside your control. [Your] life belongs to you, and it is your responsibility to make the most of it. Nobody else can do this for you."

Jonathan experienced this firsthand when he failed to make the varsity lacrosse team in his Junior year of high school. Forced to watch his classmates live the varsity fantasy while he was shut out, he struggled with a huge sense of rejection and worthlessness. His disappointment manifested as sulking and lackadaisical practice habits early in the season on the junior varsity team—not exactly the portrait of grit.

One day, his coach took him aside. "I get that you wanted to be on varsity," he said. "But you need to be where your feet are."

Jonathan realized he'd been stuck in his head, hung up on all the glory he *could* be experiencing if he was somewhere else— while forgetting that all his power lay in committing to what he had right here, right now. He shook off his funk and doubled down on practice, galvanizing his team to be successful.

Together with the other older players, Jonathan helped bring his JV team to the standards of the varsity team in terms of play style, expectations, and execution. As the season progressed and his performance rose to meet this new challenge, he and his teammates jokingly began to refer to him as the "self-proclaimed most prolific scorer in JV lacrosse history." When the season was over, he'd made massive improvements in his game and had contributed significantly to the team's success. More importantly, he restored his passion for the game and focused on his new path—building grit that made his senior year on varsity more productive, enjoyable, and meaningful.

BECOME AN EXPERT ON YOURSELF

Jonathan's breakthrough didn't just come from being gritty—it came from seeing himself clearly, thanks in part to the nudge from his coach. His coach held up a mirror, showing Jonathan a talented athlete who was wasting perfectly good training time moping when he could be taking advantage of that time to become a powerful force on that year's *and* the next year's teams. Once Jonathan tuned in to his own feelings of hurt and disappointment about not making the varsity team, he started making better decisions.

Knowing yourself is the path to self-mastery. After all, you can't really master something you don't understand—you can only *react* to it, like Jonathan did before he understood his emotions. Start studying yourself the way you would a character in a book. What pumps you up? What demoralizes you? What lifts you out of a funk? What is absolutely unacceptable to you? What will inspire you to keep pushing no matter what? Knowing yourself inside and out means you can make good decisions instead of capitulating to outside forces or your own lower instincts. Learning about yourself in this way takes time and effort. As legendary jazz musician Miles Davis said, "It took me years to learn how to play like myself."

Throughout your athletic career, plenty of people are going to have strong opinions about who you should be and what you should do: for example, your coach thinks you should wait another year to enter that competition, but your parents think you need to push now while you have the momentum. But at the end of the day, you're the person living inside your body—the one who knows how tired or stressed you feel, how confident you are, and what brings you the most excitement and joy. Self-mastery means developing the confidence to trust your own instincts, even when there's a cacophony of other voices in your head.

One tool we use frequently in our practice to help athletes find clarity about decisions is a SWOT analysis. SWOT analyses are strategic planning tools common among various industries including business and sport. SWOT stands for Strengths, Weaknesses, Opportunities, and Threats. When you do a SWOT analysis, you take an honest look at what's working for you, what's underdeveloped, what possibilities are out there, and what might get in your way of taking advantage of them.

You can use a SWOT analysis any time you're faced with a tough decision. For example, if you're deciding whether to transfer schools, your strengths might be your grades and work ethic, your weaknesses could be adjusting to new teammates, your opportunities might include better coaching or facilities, and threats could be losing playing time or scholarship money. If you're considering a position change, your strength might be that you're naturally gifted at your new position, your weakness might be that you lack endurance, your opportunity might be that the new position offers significantly more playing time, and the threat might be that you'll need to learn new skills under intense time pressure.

To do your own SWOT analysis, start by dividing a piece of paper into four quadrants. In the Strengths quadrant, brainstorm all the assets you bring to the particular situation you're facing. These could be physical attributes like speed or strength, mental attributes like good analytical skills, or emotional attributes like resilience. In the Weaknesses quadrant, brainstorm anything that is currently acting as a physical, mental, or emotional barrier: for example, an injured knee or a tendency to snap at teammates when a play doesn't go how you planned.

In the Opportunities quadrant, brainstorm everything you stand to gain from making the change you're considering: More playing time? A better scholarship? Getting to work with a coach you've long admired? Finally, in the Threats quadrant, make a list of the internal and external factors that could hinder you or get in the way of your accomplishments: for example, maybe moving to a new team would mean losing your support network or giving up the seniority you've established on your existing crew.

By completing all four quadrants of the SWOT analysis, you gain valuable insights into who you are as an athlete, helping you make decisions that align with your strengths and goals.

Here's a sample SWOT analysis for a hockey player who wants to improve her speed:

Strengths	Weaknesses
• Love for hockey and movement • Desire and determination to improve	• Summer laziness • Hard to stay focused on the most "boring" aspect of hockey (skating)
Opportunities	**Threats**
• Access to ice time and training facilities • Ability to gauge improvement at multiple camps and showcases	• Potential for overuse injuries • Not fully committing to the plan • Poor nutrition

Grit is built through thousands of tiny decisions, repeated day after day and week after week: the decision to get up when the alarm rings, run those extra laps, face the heat or cold or rain or snow, and confront the opponents who scare you the most. One act of grittiness builds on another, creating a positive cascade, until grit becomes second nature. Practicing grit is how you go from coasting by on natural talent to fully inhabiting your potential as an athlete.

SKILL TO TRY:
GRIT-BUILDING CHALLENGE

Pick one thing in your sport that you've been avoiding because it's hard, boring, or it doesn't come naturally to you. Maybe it's stretching and flexibility exercises, precision skills like hitting a target, or speed. Commit to working on this one skill every single day for two weeks. Do it for a full session, not a token few minutes. And don't leave it until the end of practice—tackle it first thing and give it your all.

By the end of two weeks, you'll have proven to yourself that you can stick with something even when it feels hard or unnatural at first. Chances are, you might have even discovered a seed of enjoyment in the practice, which will make it much easier to keep improving this skill. Let your grit feed your passion and your passion feed your grit.

Head to www.mentalitywins.com/resources for a downloadable worksheet to log your progress with the Grit-Building Challenge.

PART 4

flourish

CHAPTER 12

burnout and injuries

Sloane was a celebrated CrossFit athlete who had turned her passion into a career—but somewhere along the way, the fire had gone out. Her social media was filled with photos of her grinning ecstatically after winning competitions, but when Jonathan first met her, she looked like the living dead.

"I used to get butterflies before a big workout," she told him. "Now I feel dread. I'll sit in my car outside the gym for twenty minutes, scrolling social media on my phone, trying to talk myself into going inside." She confided that she'd developed insomnia, her resting heart rate had gone up, and she was getting injured more easily.

Jonathan and Sloane worked to address the burnout through a mixture of interventions. She began working more closely with her CrossFit coach to build recovery weeks into her training program, instead of skipping them in her quest to be competition-ready. Jonathan also encouraged Sloane to develop recovery rituals to signal the end of training and encourage both her mind and body to transition into recovery. Lastly, Jonathan worked with Sloane and her coach to introduce more unstructured play into her training.

After implementing these strategies for a solid two months, Sloane's sleep improved, her resting heart rate dropped, and her smile became genuine again. Even though the volume of her workouts de-creased, her physical and emotional health had improved so much that her key lifts actually went up.

"I didn't even realize how burned out I was until I started taking recovery seriously," she said. "Now, I couldn't even imagine going back to the way I used to train."

Burnout isn't just feeling tired or drained after a tough prac-tice—it's when your body and mind have been pushed beyond their limits so frequently and for so long that they start shutting down in protest. When you're burned out, even a whole week of sleeping for twelve hours a night and binge-watching shows on the couch doesn't recharge your battery. Even *thinking* about your sport can make you anxious, tearful, or on edge. The thing that used to give you joy and meaning now puts your whole body in fight-or-flight mode. If you've been pushing yourself to per-form at a high level for a long time, it can be terrifying to see your mind and body suddenly rebel like this.

The signs of burnout can sneak up on you gradually, or they can hit like a brick wall. Your performance starts leveling off or even declining despite maintaining your training routine. You might notice yourself losing strength or stamina, feeling ex-hausted even after rest days, or that your resting heart rate and blood pressure are higher than usual. Mentally, you might strug-gle to concentrate during practice or forget plays you've known for years.

Burnout and physical injury are closely linked. When you're mentally and emotionally exhausted, your focus suffers, making you more likely to make mistakes that lead to injury. Chronic stress also suppresses your immune system and interferes with your body's ability to repair itself, meaning you're slower to heal from the normal wear and tear of training. Plus, when you're burned out, you're more likely to ignore your body's warning signs and push through pain that should signal you to rest. It's a vicious cycle—burnout leads to injury, and injury can worsen burnout as you deal with the frustration of being sidelined.

But perhaps the most telling sign is what happens to your relationship with your sport. That activity that used to make you jump out of bed on game day suddenly feels like an appointment for a root canal. You might find yourself dreading practice, making excuses to skip workouts, or avoiding the places, objects, and people you associate with your sport. You might feel angry, sad, or high-strung, snapping at people you care about and then feeling mortified by your own behavior. In the midst of it all, you might have the feeling that you're not allowed to slow down, let alone quit—that you're stuck on a high-speed treadmill with no "off" button.

In 2021, Naomi Osaka was the number two tennis player in the world, a two-time winner of both the Australian Open and U.S. Open, and being hailed by the media as "the next Serena or Venus Williams." But behind the endorsement deals and tournament victories, she was experiencing classic burnout symptoms. Journalists' aggressive questioning at press conferences clashed with her reserved personality and traditional Japanese cultural values. She felt more like a lottery ticket than a human being—an object on which other peoples' hopes were riding, with no regard for her own feelings. For years, she'd been feeling intense anxiety before games, accompanied by heavy depression.

In the early days of the French Open, Osaka announced she'd be skipping postgame press conferences, as the intense questioning negatively impacted her mental health, especially when journalists honed in on mistakes she had made. This ignited a furor, with officials slapping on a $15,000 fine and threatening to expel her from the tournament if she refused to fulfill her "media obligations." As a result, Osaka decided to drop out of the French Open and step away from tennis to focus on her mental health.

When Osaka returned to competition, her ranking had dropped, and she hadn't won any major tournaments. Some critics pointed to this as evidence that her break had been a mistake. But this misses the point entirely. Osaka herself has said that her new approach to tennis has made the sport more enjoyable and her career more sustainable. She chose long-term health over short-term results—exactly what athletes struggling with burnout should do.

Osaka's example demonstrates that it's possible to step back, get help, and return to competition on your own terms. Sometimes the most courageous thing you can do is admit you need a break, even when the world is telling you to keep pushing through. After all, what good is it to become an elite athlete if you wake up each day wanting to crawl under a rock and hide?

Kim's journey to becoming a sport clinician was profoundly influenced by a devastating experience in college when her roommate, a fellow athlete, died by suicide. Kim had struggled with depression for years, and seeing a person so similar to herself die from mental health-related challenges shook her to her core. This experience made Kim realize that depression, burnout, and other mental health issues are not minor problems in sports but life-threatening conditions for athletes who often face intense pressures in and out of sport. She now devotes a significant portion of her work to suicide prevention, as well as counseling athletes who have lost a teammate to suicide—and she places just as much importance on her own mental health as she does on her physical condition.

Although we tend to associate sports with physical injuries like sprained wrists and shin splints, the truth is that emotional and psychological injuries are just as common. When you're under constant pressure to perform—dealing with complex and sometimes intense interpersonal dynamics with teammates and coaches—and struggling to balance your athletic career with school, work, and family responsibilities, taking care of your mental health is just as important as resting and icing those sprained joints.

RISK AND PROTECTIVE FACTORS

There's a handful of factors that make burnout and mental health challenges more likely. First, there's overtraining without adequate recovery. In our eagerness to become stronger and faster, we forget that our bodies aren't machines (and neither, for that matter, are our minds). We ask tiny muscle groups to do more than they were designed for, aggravating them to the point of injury, or we push ourselves to memorize play after play until our brains shut down in protest. We adopt a "more-is-better" attitude to training, not realizing that by doing so, we're robbing ourselves of the rest we need to be healthy and happy. In our rush to train twenty-four hours a day, we stop doing the *other* things that make us happy, like making art, spending time with friends, or playing with pets.

Another major contributor to burnout is pressure from coaches, parents, teammates, or the media. There can be a fine line between pressure and encouragement. Sometimes, even the person doing the pressuring believes they are "just being

encouraging." Encouragement turns to pressure when it prior-
itizes the pusher's agenda, not your lived reality, and when the
word "no" feels like disappointing someone. When another person's career or sense of self is riding on your performance, you
can end up pushing yourself way past your limits to please them.
If this goes on for too long, you can start to feel like a horse
that's being used to drag someone else's chariot—desperate to
rest but endlessly urged to keep going.

Coaches sometimes use "tough love" to motivate athletes,
but in some cases, this can cross a line into bullying or harass-
ment. Ask yourself if coaches and others in your life are truly encouraging you, or if they're trying to extract as much as possible
from you while ignoring your humanity. Do your coaches and
teammates still support you if you're sick or injured? Do they
encourage you to cultivate your relationships, your creativity,
and your spirituality? Or do they try to claim 100 percent of you,
not just within your sport, but your whole life?

As we discussed in Chapter 10, perfectionism is another
major culprit in driving burnout, depression, and anxiety. When
your entire sense of safety and self-worth is riding on doing one
specific skill perfectly, you're skating on thin ice. The more you
believe that your life is *over* if you ever stop being the best, the
more at risk you are. Perfectionism gives you tunnel vision and
stops you from seeing what's obvious to everyone else: that your
life will be just fine without this sport or without doing this sport
at this level of perfection.

Just as there are risk factors, there are also some factors
that can *protect* you from burnout. Having strong relationships
with family, friends, and teammates who support you as a person—not just as an athlete—is extremely protective. These are
the people who celebrate holidays with you, snuggle up on the
couch and watch movies with you, and ask about your pets and

hobbies, not just your latest results. They can give you the out-side perspective you need to remember that you have worth be-yond just being able to execute a Yurchenko double pike—you're also a funny, loyal, and beloved human.

Having interests outside of your sport helps too—whether that's an art or craft like painting or woodworking, a mind-body practice like tai chi, or volunteer work that puts you in touch with a higher purpose. Using your body to do something *other* than perform your sport—and your mind to do something other than analyzing that performance—reminds you that "athlete" is just one aspect of your identity, not the whole thing. Even if you spend serious hours on training and competition, make a point of carving out at least an hour a week to engage in this other hobby.

During the hours when you *are* engaged in your sport, focus on the process, not the outcome. Stay present and enjoy the moment. Find pleasure in everyday things like improving your skills, noticing the beauty or excitement of the places where you get to train or compete, enjoying how good your food tastes after an intense workout, and appreciating how well you sleep when you're totally spent. These things have nothing to do with winning or losing—they're about the pleasure of being in an ac-tive body, enjoying all that it means to be human in this world.

Finally, treat rest, recovery, and play as essential compo-nents of your training. Build those things into your schedule—actually write them down on your calendar and stick to them. Never treat them as optional, because they're not. If you strug-gle to feel that you "deserve" mental or physical rest, or feel like less-intense days are a "waste," work with a sport clinician to challenge those beliefs before you do lasting damage to your physical or mental health. *Everyone* deserves play, rest, and re-covery, and these things should never be contingent on your performance.

OVERCOMING STIGMA

Although "go see a therapist" may seem like obvious advice, all too many athletes feel squeamish about seeking help for burn-out and other mental health challenges. One of Kim's athletes only met with Kim because her mom arranged a surprise session after suspecting her daughter had an eating disorder. Earlier, this athlete had survived a devastating accident in a ski race that landed her in the hospital. The eating disorder felt like a way of regaining a sliver of control as she went through a barrage of surgeries that made her feel like everything familiar to her was spiraling away.

After a few sessions of discussing her eating habits, she and Kim uncovered just how much the ski accident had affected her. She had insomnia, intrusive images, and nightmares. She had come to rely on the eating disorder to suppress her mood swings and held on to it like a life preserver. She was convinced that she did not belong in the world and begged for a way out.

Today, this athlete credits therapy for saving her life—and her mom for having both the perceptiveness and courage to call in someone to help when she was drowning. She says, "I would not be here if not for all those who held my hand and stood in my corner through the storms and never-ending days."

Perhaps the biggest barrier athletes face to accessing mental health care is stigma. Not only do we still live in a world where seeking help is sometimes seen as "soft" or "weak," but athletes are often stereotyped as being immune to things like anxiety and depression. After all, how can a person who's fearless on the ice or in the wrestling ring need *therapy*? As the celebrated swimmer Michael Phelps said, "For the longest time, I thought asking for help was a sign of weakness because that's kind of what society teaches us. That's especially true from an athlete's perspective.

If we ask for help, then we're not this big macho athlete that people can look up to. Well, you know what? If someone wants to call me weak for asking for help, that's their problem. Because I'm saving my own life."

Plenty of athletes worry that publicly admitting to anxiety, depression, or other mental health challenges will make their teammates and coaches lose confidence in their ability to compete. And some athletes have even bought into the belief that success comes at the expense of healthy emotional coping—in other words, that having your sport make you feel angry or depressed is just the price you pay for playing at a high level. This mindset creates fertile ground for burnout because it leads you to ignore the recovery, rest, and self-care you need to be physically and emotionally well.

The truth is, taking care of your mental health is essential to a long, successful career as an athlete—indeed, it may be one of the most important ingredients to lasting success. The risk of serious mental health problems or even suicide is very real, as Kim and Jonathan know all too well from working with athletes at every level. In fact, all athletes should have a crisis plan—a document identifying people you can go to for support, including friends, coaches, teammates, and professionals like a therapist or psychologist. Although it's easy to tell yourself, "I'll never need that," this kind of planning means that if you *do* get deeply distressed or suicidal, you are much more likely to get the support you need quickly. You can find a sample crisis plan online at www.suicidesafetyplan.com.

Be proactive about your mental health. You don't need to wait until you're in crisis to reach out to a therapist. In fact, having an established relationship with a sport clinician can stop you from getting to a crisis point in the first place. Just as you would prevent a physical injury by taking the time to stretch and consulting a physiotherapist, working with a sport clinician throughout your athletic career can save you from the most common mental and emotional injuries that athletes suffer.

DEALING WITH INJURIES

In the case of the ski racer who worked with Kim, a devastating injury was the catalyst for her eating disorder and accompanying depression—and she is far from alone. Injuries are one of the most common triggers for mental health issues among athletes. One moment, you're sailing toward the season you envisioned, working toward goals you hold dear, and the next moment you're in pain, sidelined to the bench, all your hopes and expectations shattered. You might feel intense grief, as the injury leads to a temporary loss of self—not to mention missing out on milestones and experiences you were looking forward to. You might feel anger and frustration at sitting things out while the rest of your team gets to keep moving forward. And when you finally *do* recover, you might feel intense trepidation about returning to your sport. After all, what if you get injured again? Or what if your injury set you back so far that it feels hopeless to even try again?

The key is to treat recovery like a sport. Remind yourself you're still an athlete—your training is just going to look very different for a while. Adopting this mindset will help you find the motivation you need to not only stay positive throughout the recovery process, but build new mental skills that will help you when you get back to your "real" sport.

As devastating as an injury may be, injuries can also bring about a lot of positive psychological changes. For example, many injured athletes develop a finer awareness of their body after an injury because they've spent months focusing on specific muscles or movements. This heightened awareness continues to serve them long after their injury has healed. It can even be preventative against future injuries, as they can now detect the subtle changes that warn that this body part is getting aggravated.

Injuries are also a great opportunity to work on skills like mindfulness and focus that can dramatically improve your performance once you're back in the game. Even if you're stuck on the couch, you can still work on present-moment awareness, mental rehearsal, and visualization. In fact, you can potentially log *more* hours training using only your imagination than you could when you were cleared to play in real life! If you're the kind of person who tends to put off mental practice, this can be exactly the opportunity you need to discover just how powerful it is.

Although burnout and injuries may make you feel like you've hit a dead end, neither of these conditions are finish lines (unless you want them to be). Not only are they treatable, but living through them and coming out the other side can help you to develop skills and potential that might have otherwise gone unrealized. These conditions can make you question your very identity, and that's a *good* thing if you can engage with the question thoughtfully and with solid support. Perhaps most importantly, burnout and injuries teach you to respect your own humanity at the deepest level so you can flourish both on the field and off.

SKILL TO TRY: INJURY MANTRA

Creating a mantra related to your injury can be a helpful way to keep you grounded when you experience frustration or setbacks. An injury mantra is a simple word or a phrase that helps guide you through your recovery and reminds you that you are resilient and will emerge stronger through this experience. Come up with a mantra that feels hopeful, confident, and natural to you. Some examples of injury mantras include:

- Strength through struggle
- I can, and will, make it through this
- There are better days ahead
- One day at a time
- I am resilient, I am strong

Write your mantra in a place you will see it every day, like your phone lock screen, bathroom mirror, or water bottle. When you feel frustrated or hopeless, repeat your mantra until you feel more at ease.

self-compassion and self-acceptance

Maya was a sixteen-year-old figure skater whose routines were seemingly perfect—every jump landed, every spin centered. But no matter how well Maya performed or how warmly the audience applauded, she felt sad and empty inside.

When Kim started working with Maya, she discovered that years of harsh coaching had taught Maya to see herself as worthless, lazy, and contemptible. When other skaters fell during practice, Maya felt sympathy. When she fell, she felt only disgust. When she saw other athletes eating meals after competition, she was envious that they were nourishing their bodies. When she ate anything at all, she punished herself for her lack of self-discipline.

"I basically hate myself," Maya said. "And even though I feel a drive to win, I don't take pleasure in winning—instead, I immediately find the next thing that's wrong with me to focus on."

Kim's work with Maya centered on helping her see that the same compassion she showed to others could be turned toward herself. This shift didn't happen overnight. Maya was so used to seeing herself as an unruly force that could only be kept in check with constant harshness

and criticism that she literally couldn't imagine being kind to herself.
She had to learn to sit with difficult emotions—disappointment, frus-
tration, fear—without immediately turning them into weapons in the
never-ending war to keep herself in line. It took years, but finally,
Maya began to feel a seed of compassion for herself.

"Befriending myself was the most radical thing I've ever done in
my life," Maya later told Kim. "The biggest, most beautiful act of re-
bellion I can imagine. I don't know what would have happened to me
if I hadn't done it."

Although most of us grew up with the understanding that we should be compassionate toward others, few of us were ever taught to show consistent and radical compassion toward ourselves—especially if we were raised to be "tough, invincible" athletes. When you saw another kid crying on the playground, you probably ran over to comfort them, but when you were the one with a scraped knee, you tried hard *not* to cry. As you grew up, you might have received messages from coaches and teachers that "real" athletes are hard on themselves and "don't make excuses." Is it any surprise that so many of us end up like Maya—presenting a flawless exterior but suffering intensely on the inside?

In our sport psychology practices, we often work with athletes who can't even fathom what it would feel like to be kind to themselves. For better or for worse, we've both been there too—caught in the illusion that having talent in a sport means you need to be strict, relentless, and harsh with yourself or run the risk of falling off.

Jonathan's parents met on a blind date to play tennis, and the sport quickly became the family religion. Summer mornings on Martha's Vineyard meant piling into the car at dawn, a basket of yellow balls rattling in the trunk, heading to the local courts for epic family doubles matches—one parent and kid versus the other parent and kid.

Those were magical times. The only things that could stop their games were the morning donut run or, in the evenings, the swarms of bugs drawn to the court lights. Jonathan got really good. He started winning local tournaments and felt like he'd found his calling, managing to hang with players everyone considered elite, even when he didn't always come out on top.

But in his quest to become a star, Jonathan started being harder and harder on himself. Every missed shot became a threat to his sense of self. The court became a theater for his rage—yelling, screaming, broken rackets, you name it. As the competition intensified and expectations mounted, so did his fury. The sport that had once brought his family together was now tearing him apart from the inside.

By high school, Jonathan had made one of the hardest decisions of his young life: he quit tennis. The weight of being singularly responsible for every point won or lost had become too much for his adolescent mind to bear. It was heartbreaking to walk away from something that had defined him for so long, but his relationship with the sport had become too unhealthy. He didn't know then what he knows now—that self-compassion, not self-flagellation, is the key to longevity as an athlete.

Now, as an adult athlete, Jonathan works constantly on incorporating more self-compassion into his relationship with himself. As he has aged, sports have become more enjoyable, and his performance in sports like running and golf has improved. Instead of beating himself up and running his body into the ground, he has a better understanding of what he truly values about these sports. He now sees sports as a celebration of life and a great way to connect with family and friends, not a must-win situation. If he could time-travel back to his teenaged years, he would tell himself to learn self-compassion right away instead of waiting until he was grown.

WHAT IS SELF-COMPASSION?

Self-compassion means showing yourself kindness and under-standing, even when you're feeling frustrated or disappointed, and setting appropriate goals and expectations for yourself in-stead of holding yourself to impossible standards that are guar-anteed to make you fall short.

When some athletes hear words like "self-compassion," they think it means letting yourself off the hook or slacking off in your training. They worry that being kind to yourself will make you soft and lose your competitive edge—or maybe even give up on a demanding sport entirely. If this is you, we want to reassure you that self-compassion doesn't mean lowering your standards or making excuses; it means supporting yourself sincerely and effectively while you reach for those high standards.

In her book *Self-Compassion: The Proven Power of Being Kind to Yourself,* Kristen Neff, leading self-compassion researcher and practitioner, discusses three main components of self-compas-sion. These are self-kindness vs. self-judgment, common hu-manity vs. isolation, and mindfulness vs. over-identification.

The first, self-kindness vs. self-judgment, emphasizes the importance of being kind and understanding toward yourself when you encounter adversity. Picture the best coach or cap-tain you ever had. How did that person help you and encourage you through obstacles? Did they use supportive words? Or show acts of kindness, like bringing you a hot chocolate after practice? Did they help you put things in perspective and remember the bigger picture when you were spiraling? Did they remind you of your strengths instead of tearing you down for your weaknesses? Self-kindness means treating yourself exactly the same way.

The second element of self-compassion, common humanity vs. isolation, encourages us to remember that failure and imperfection are part of being human. Having a bad practice or performance is not a sign that you're uniquely weak or flawed—on the contrary, it's a sign you have something in common with every other person who has ever walked this earth. When we fail, we often feel like we're alone, when we're actually in very good company. Just think of all the athletes you admire who have come back from spectacular snafus. When you see the common humanity in your situation, you can let your suffering connect you rather than separate you from others, making it easier to bounce back from adversity.

The third aspect of self-compassion Neff describes, mindfulness vs. over-identification, is the ability to keep perspective on difficult situations. When you overidentify with a mistake, you tend to do one of two things: either blow it out of proportion and act like it's the worst thing that has ever happened to you, or, the opposite, act like it didn't really happen or didn't affect you at all. By approaching the situation mindfully, you can see it for what it is and take appropriate steps to resolve it instead of going straight to an inappropriate extreme. You can say, "OK, that thing happened, but it's not the end of my life. It's not the end of my career. It's not even the end of my season."

When you practice all three elements on a consistent basis, you will stay balanced in the midst of uncertainty instead of spinning out and feeling like the sky is falling. You will actually *enjoy* your sport, finding joy and meaning in the process, because the heaviness of impossible expectations will no longer be weighing you down. Although self-judgment can feel like an effective spur in the short term, only self-compassion will let you thrive as an athlete in the long term.

THE RAIN METHOD FOR BUILDING SELF-COMPASSION

One of our favorite techniques to teach athletes who struggle with self-compassion is the RAIN method, developed by spiritual teacher and psychologist Tara Brach. RAIN stands for Recognize, Allow, Investigate, and Nurture.

It starts with taking a moment to **recognize** the emotion you are feeling by naming that emotion out loud or in your head—for example, "I'm feeling super disappointed about losing that race right now."

Once you've recognized the emotion you're feeling, the next step is to simply **allow** it to be there. If you're feeling disappointed about the race, let yourself feel disappointed! Don't try to rush or force that emotion to change. This practice teaches you that emotions come and go—they're not fires that need to be put out the moment they start smoldering.

Once you've fully accepted the existence of your emotion, **investigate** the emotion in greater detail. Where in your body do you feel this emotion? Is it tingly, achy, heavy, or sharp? What kind of thoughts or images go along with it? How much space is it taking up in your awareness? The simple practice of investigating your emotion gives you a little distance from it and reminds you that your life is bigger than this temporary feeling. It also activates your prefrontal cortex (the part of your brain responsible for awareness, perspective, and emotion regulation) and this cools down your initial reactivity.

Once you've given suitable time to this investigation, the last step is to **nurture** yourself. Sitting with unwanted emotions can be uncomfortable, to say the least, and this step is all about soothing your nervous system. If you're in the middle of a game or performance, this could mean taking a deep breath or repeating a mantra—and if you're at home, it could mean taking a walk, petting your dog, coloring, journaling, or doing another activity that helps you feel the opposite of that unwanted emotion you are experiencing.

The beauty of RAIN for athletes is that it gives you a reliable framework for dealing with the emotional rollercoaster that comes with competitive sports. Instead of bottling up your frustration after a bad game, letting it completely derail your confidence for weeks, or punishing yourself with harsh judgment, RAIN teaches you how to process those feelings in real time. When you can move through all four steps smoothly, you develop the kind of emotional resilience that keeps you competing at your best, even when things don't go your way.

Over time, this practice doesn't just help you handle setbacks better—it makes you more emotionally available for the joy and satisfaction that comes with sports. Feeling your emotions fully ensures that you don't get "stuck" in them. When you can effectively process the inevitable stress, disappointment, and embarrassment that can arise during sports, you make space for positive emotions to surface in their place.

SELF-ACCEPTANCE

Self-compassion goes hand in hand with another important emotional skill: self-acceptance. Self-acceptance is the practice of accepting all your attributes, positive or negative, without judgment.

As an athlete, you're always pursuing some kind of intense goal, whether it's making the team, making it to the Olympics or Paralympics, winning a medal, or simply beating your personal best. It's normal and perhaps inevitable to start conflating the achievement of these goals with your self-worth—to let the disappointment of not winning a game turn into disappointment with yourself as a human being. Keeping those two things separate requires a great deal of psychological and emotional skill, and those skills aren't automatic—we need to learn and practice them.

You can start to develop self-acceptance by taking a deep dive into the stories of athletes you admire. The more you learn about people like Simone Biles, Lionel Messi, and Trischa Zorn, the more you realize that every single one of them has faced devastating losses, injuries, and moments when they questioned whether they were good enough. If these sporting giants aren't exempt from the disappointment inherent in athletics, why should you be? When you truly understand that struggle is a normal part of sports, you realize your weaknesses are normal and surmountable, too.

Another crucial self-acceptance practice is to appreciate your body and mind for what they *can* do, not just criticizing them for what they can't do *yet*. Athletes are notorious for focusing intensely on weaknesses, flaws, and areas that need improvement. This is useful for refining your goals and fine-tuning your training regimen, but it turns into a problem when it becomes the only lens through which you view yourself.

Every day, make a point of acknowledging the incredible things your body does for you: the speed of your legs, the strength of your arms, the dependability of your heart beating, and your lungs pulling in air. Notice what feels easy, wonderful, and fun. Also pay attention to the moments when your mind serves you well—when you stay calm under pressure, make good tactical decisions, and practice gratitude. Realize that you're *already doing* amazing things—you don't need to wait for some far-off future to feel good about yourself.

Finally, even though your current struggle may be hogging nearly all your mental real estate, try to zoom out and look at it within the context of your entire athletic journey. When you're in a rut or dealing with an injury, it can feel like this moment defines everything about you as an athlete. But this is just one chapter in a much longer story.

Remind yourself of all the times you've overcome difficulties before, starting with that time in second grade when you were the only one in your class who didn't know how to skate and had to hold on to the back of a chair. The fact that you experienced adversity in the past but still went on to become the athlete you are today should be all the proof you need that setbacks do not define you. In fact, when you look back at the experiences that felt like disasters, you might even laugh or smile when you realize how little they affected you in the long run.

If you've been cut off from your own needs and feelings after years of high-pressure coaching or self-imposed expectations, self-compassion and self-acceptance can be your bridge back to a healthy relationship with yourself. At the end of your life, will you be glad you subjugated your humanity in the name of running fast or doing fancy moves on a snowboard? Or will you wish you'd let yourself experience happiness, connection, and love, regardless of whether you continued to be elite? Remember, you only have one life to live—so make sure you're enjoying it, not just succeeding at it.

SKILL TO TRY:
THREE COMPASSION PRACTICES

Here are three ways to build compassion:

- Think about or write down a failure you have had in your life that you are grateful for. What did you learn from this failure, and how has it encouraged you to respond to yourself with kindness and unconditional love in the future?

- Make a commitment to spending two minutes three times per day (morning, midday, evening) reflecting on the distinction between yourself and your performance. Remind yourself in those moments that judging yourself and your performance as "good" or "bad" is not a helpful way to learn and grow as an athlete and a human being.

- Extend compassion to your teammates, especially when they make mistakes. Practice separating your thoughts and feelings about the mistake they made from their worth as a person and make a point of speaking to them with support and kindness after it happens.

CHAPTER 14

values, identity, and leadership

Elijah was a Division I basketball player who'd always been known as a respectful, family-oriented kid growing up in a tight-knit commu-nity in Ohio. Basketball had given him a full scholarship to a small but prestigious college, and his two younger brothers looked up to him as their role model. But by the middle of his sophomore season, Elijah was barely recognizable to the people who knew him best. He started blowing off family gatherings, going to parties several nights a week, and showing up to practice either hungover or still buzzed from the night before.

He seemed to revel in the social status that came with being on the basketball team—that thrill of walking down the hallways and feeling like a god—but to his close friends, he had become arrogant, snobby, and even a little bit mean. His coach had already given him two formal warnings about his partying, and his playing time had been reduced significantly.

When Elijah first met with Jonathan, he was defensive and dis-missive. "I'm just blowing off steam," he said. "College is supposed to be fun, right? Everyone parties." But as they continued talking, it became clear that Elijah felt completely disconnected from himself. The pressure of maintaining his scholarship, combined with being away from home for the first time, had left him feeling lost and overwhelmed. Rather than dealing with these feelings directly, he leaned on minor thrills to keep himself going.

Jonathan worked with Elijah to identify what had been most important to him before college. Elijah realized that his core values included respect for others, being a positive role model for his siblings, and maintaining close family relationships. When Jonathan asked Elijah to rate how well his current behavior aligned with these values on a scale of 1 to 10, Elijah quietly admitted it was probably . . . a 3. "I don't even recognize myself anymore," he said. "My little brother called me last week all excited to tell me about making JV, and I was so hungover I could barely focus on what he was saying. That's not who I want to be."

Together, they developed a plan to help Elijah reconnect with his values. Elijah committed to calling home twice a week at times when he would be clear-headed and present. He also decided to limit his partying to weekends only and never the night before practice or games. Most importantly, Elijah began to see how his behavior toward his old friends was risking ruining decades-long relationships.

Over the course of several months, Elijah noticed that as his actions became more aligned with his values, he felt more like himself again. His coach noticed the change too, gradually increasing his playing time. More importantly, his relationship with his family had been restored. "I realized that trying to escape from pressure by acting like someone I'm not just created more pressure," Elijah reflected. "When I started acting like the person I actually want to be, everything got easier, including basketball."

Values are the beliefs that guide you as a person, both in and out of sport. They're the qualities you most treasure in yourself—the things you want people to remember about you long after you're gone. Do you want to be remembered for your honesty? Your kindness? Your devotion to your family? Your work ethic? Your refusal to give up? This is a sign that you value these things deeply. They're core to who you are, and although you might drift away from them now and then, you will always want to return to them when you realize you've gone off course.

Although we receive many of our values from our family of origin, we continue to refine them throughout our teenage years and adulthood, often rejecting some of the ones that were handed to us by our parents while embracing new ones. For example, maybe when you were a teenager, you swore that you'd *never* choose security over freedom, and that you'd put loyalty to your friends above all else. As an adult, you might have added values like standing up for people who are vulnerable or always doing your best.

When you know your values, you can make choices that align with what you believe in. You know what you stand for, and that creates a sort of filter on reality. If you value honesty, you're not going to cheat on a test or feel comfortable with friends who do. If you value collaboration, you'll find ways to support your teammates even when it means giving up on some personal glory. Having clear values is like having a flashlight on your path, showing you the right thing to do in every situation.

When you speak, act, and live in alignment with your values, you're more likely to feel good about the choices you make. In contrast, when you don't live and play according to your values, you experience cognitive dissonance—the mental tension that arises when the things you do don't match up to the beliefs you profess. You might also feel a nagging sense of guilt or shame about the decisions you've made and the person you've become.

Even if you're outwardly successful, these negative feelings can ultimately make you feel depressed or like an imposter. You know deep down that this isn't who you want to be or how you want to live. Like Elijah, you may even realize that you stand to lose friendships and relationships that mean everything to you—and that you don't even recognize *yourself* anymore. This disconnect between your values and your actions doesn't just affect your sense of identity—it also damages your self-esteem. When you consistently act against what you believe in, it becomes harder to respect yourself or trust your own judgment. Healthy self-esteem, on the other hand, comes from living in alignment with the values you hold dear.

BUILDING HEALTHY SELF-ESTEEM

Healthy self-esteem is an important but often-overlooked aspect of thriving in sports. When you feel good about yourself, you're more likely to go for the winning shot, while someone with low self-esteem might play it safe—or self-sabotage by taking a risky shot they have no hope of making. You're also more likely to live according to your values instead of giving into outside pressure because you're not trying to put on a show for people or turn into someone you're not.

In his book *The Six Pillars of Self-Esteem*, psychotherapist Nathaniel Branden emphasizes six core practices that contribute to an individual's self-esteem: living consciously, self-acceptance, self-responsibility, self-assertiveness, living purposefully, and personal integrity. Let's take a look at each one of these in more detail to see how they pertain to you as an athlete.

LIVING CONSCIOUSLY

Living consciously means refusing to sleepwalk through life and instead becoming an active participant in everything you do, both on and off the athletic field. A conscious athlete pays attention to their self-talk, notices when they're getting distracted, and engages with their experience, whether they're having a great practice or slogging through a difficult one. Living consciously gives you a sense of agency and self-respect you just can't get by tuning out and coasting.

SELF-ACCEPTANCE

As we discussed in Chapter 13, self-acceptance means embracing your strengths and weaknesses as a normal part of being human. This doesn't mean settling for mediocrity. An athlete with healthy self-acceptance can admit when they made a mistake without spiraling into self-hatred. They can recognize they're not the fastest runner on the team while still valuing their contribution. When you accept yourself, you stop wasting energy in useless self-flagellation and keep your eye on the bigger picture.

SELF-RESPONSIBILITY

Athletes who practice self-responsibility own their training, performance, and emotional reactions. They don't blame coaches, teammates, the weather, or the referee. They show up to practice ready to work, take care of their body through proper nutrition and sleep, and respond to setbacks by asking "What can I learn from this?" rather than "Who can I blame?" Self-responsibility boosts your self-esteem because it places your development as an athlete firmly into your own hands.

SELF-ASSERTIVENESS

Self-assertiveness means standing up for your needs, boundaries, and values. This might mean having an awkward conversation with your coach about playing time, speaking up when an aspect of team culture is having a negative impact on you, or maintaining your training standards even when your teammates slack off. When you're self-assertive, you don't wait for others to stand up for you or advocate for your needs—you trust yourself to do that work skillfully and well. This in turn leads to increased respect from others, creating a positive cycle.

LIVING PURPOSEFULLY

Living purposefully means understanding your "why"—whether it's your love of movement, your passion for inspiring others, or the joy of seeing what you can do. This purpose guides your daily choices, from waking up early for practice to volunteering with the Special Olympics on weekends to giving up fast food (or eating more fast food, depending on your situation!). When you have a strong purpose, temporary disappointments don't throw you off because you *know* it's worth it to you to keep pushing through.

PERSONAL INTEGRITY

Integrity means aligning your actions with your stated values—otherwise known as walking your talk. If you say teamwork matters, you support your teammates even when they're competing for your position. If you claim to want excellence, you give your best effort in practice, not just during games. Athletes who live with integrity follow through on commitments to coaches and teammates, compete fairly, and maintain their character under pressure. This pillar builds trust with others and, crucially, with yourself—you become someone you can depend on, which forms the foundation of unshakeable confidence.

———

When these six pillars are in place, you become an athlete who not only has physical talent but also a solid psychological foundation for success. You also protect yourself from the negative impacts that go along with low self-esteem, like substance abuse, eating disorders, and accepting abusive treatment from others. Healthy self-esteem means knowing your worth and insisting that others treat you as worthy, too.

BECOMING AN IMPACTFUL LEADER

Building healthy self-esteem sets you up to be an impactful leader in your sport. After all, when you feel good about yourself, you're naturally better at inspiring the people around you. Confidence is contagious, and modeling qualities like self-assertiveness and personal integrity can set the tone for the rest of your team. Think about the best leaders you've known—like coaches or team captains. They probably made you feel like you belonged, that your contributions mattered, and that they had your back. They stood up for the team when it was called for and weren't afraid to have difficult conversations when someone wasn't pulling their weight.

One of Jonathan's best coaches was Lars, his childhood tennis instructor from the revered Sportsmen's Tennis Club in Boston. Jonathan used to get picked on by other kids because he would cry and get upset when they made fun of him. One day, Lars took Jonathan aside. With a combination of warmth and sternness, he said, "You need to stand up for yourself and stop letting those kids take your lunch money." The more they talked, the more Jonathan realized that the reason he was letting the other kids walk all over him was because he had low self-esteem. Once he started respecting himself, his self-worth exploded. He started biting back verbally at the other kids and stopped being an easy target. Even though Lars taught Jonathan countless things about tennis that made him a better player, what Jonathan carried with him into adulthood was the lesson about defending his self-worth.

While all leaders have their own unique way of guiding others, people tend to fall into one of four basic leadership styles: motivational, transformational, relational, and service-oriented. Jonathan's tennis coach was a prime example of a motivational coach, who rallied Jonathan to dig deep and find the self-respect he needed to stand up to the other kids.

Understanding these leadership styles can help you recognize your natural tendencies as a leader and develop the skills that don't come as naturally to you. Let's take a closer look at each one:

- *Motivational leaders* encourage teammates to push themselves to the limit and have the biggest impact in competitions. They can be vocal and/or lead by example in their work ethic, commitment, and determination: Think of U.S. soccer player Megan Rapinoe inspiring her teammates through her fearless playing style and courageousness in stepping up for penalty kicks, or NFL player Ray Lewis' legendary pregame speeches.

- *Transformational leaders* inspire others by creating and promoting a shared vision for the team. Think of how head coach Steve Kerr transformed the Golden State Warriors through his vision of "beautiful basketball," rallying them to play with joy, flow, and freedom, or how Billie Jean King revolutionized tennis through her vision of women's equality in sports.

- *Relational leaders* emphasize the importance of positive relationships among teammates. They cultivate an inclusive environment with open communication, listening, trust building, empowerment, and collaboration among all members. WNBA player Sue Bird exemplified a relational leadership style, making a point of befriending each player and often acting as a diplomat between them. Her relational style is also reflected in the record she holds for the most assists in WNBA history—more than 3,000!

- *Service-oriented leaders* prioritize the needs of their team above their own. They are empathic and ethical and focus on fostering a supportive and team-oriented environment. Tim Duncan of the San Antonio Spurs is a great example of a service-oriented leader. After his teammate Manu Ginóbili had a bad performance, Duncan called him over and over until Ginóbili finally answered the phone, then invited him to dinner. He also took multiple pay cuts to allow the team to re-sign key players.

Whichever style of leadership comes naturally to you, you're going to need to cultivate a handful of core skills to thrive as a team captain or in another leadership position. Let's take a quick look at each one:

Effective communication. This means being clear and direct while staying respectful, whether you're giving feedback to a teammate or relaying team concerns to your coach. Good leaders know how to tailor their communication style to different people and situations—for example, you might be sympathetic and encouraging with a struggling player but take a more direct tone when confronting a teammate about slacking off.

Advocating for others. As a leader, you may need to advocate for less vocal or confident players or even stand up for a player who's being bullied. This sometimes means sticking your neck out when others are too afraid to do so and dealing with any fallout that occurs.

Active listening. This means reflecting back what people are telling you, asking follow-up questions, and demonstrating that you understand their concerns, not just saying you do. When teammates come to you with problems, they want to feel deeply heard and understood.

Motivating others. Motivating your teammates means understanding their deepest values and most cherished goals. Maybe one player needs to be reminded of how much they've improved since last season, and another one needs to be given props for their work ethic. Being deeply attuned to each teammate makes you more effective at helping them when they struggle or lose focus.

Creating cohesion. As a leader, you need to contribute to the sense that your team is a unified whole, not a collection of loose parts. This means organizing team activities, creating a culture in which everyone celebrates each other's victories, and resolving conflicts before they have a chance to undermine team unity.

Handling tough situations with integrity. When issues like racism, classism, homophobia, or plain old grudges and rivalries threaten to sour team culture, your job as a leader is to do the right thing, even if it means giving up wins or sanctioning key players. This shows more vulnerable players that you're not going to betray them just to make it to the championship.

Developing these leadership skills isn't just about becoming a better captain—it's about living out your values in action. When you communicate with integrity, advocate for others, and shape your team's culture, you're not just fulfilling a role; you're expressing who you are and what you stand for. And when you can do this authentically, you feel happier and healthier at every level.

Although we live and express our values in all aspects of life, sports have a special way of forcing us to clarify what really matters to us and hold fast to those things under pressure. Sports strip away the abstract nature of values and make them concrete. Do you throw your teammate under the bus so that you can advance, or do you stand up for them? Do you do your best when nobody's watching, or do you take every possible chance to slack off? Are you truly proud of who you are, or are you letting others take advantage of your self-doubt to influence you? Getting clear on your values and leading with them is the secret to feeling good in your own skin, both in sports and in life.

SKILL TO TRY: LEADERSHIP REFLECTION

Becoming a great leader involves a lot of critical self-reflection. One reflective journaling exercise, inspired by Kim's experience with the University of Michigan's Sport Social Work Program, involves asking yourself five key questions:

1) Why do I lead?
2) Why do I lead in the way that I do?
3) What does it feel like to be led by me?
4) Is my leadership worth imitating?
5) What do I want to accomplish as a leader?

Try writing or thinking about each of these questions in depth, and consider what changes you can make to live out your leadership potential.

Head to www.mentalitywins.com/resources for a downloadable Leadership Reflection worksheet with prompts on your leadership experiences, values, and goals.

conclusion

As you finish this book, remember this fundamental truth: once your physical preparation reaches a certain threshold, it's your mental game that determines whether you truly thrive as an athlete.

Once you can run or swim or skate or wrestle or swing a golf club at a high level, your mentality becomes your biggest competitive advantage. Can you stay calm under pressure? Can you tap into your values to motivate yourself? Can you reach out for help when you need it instead of letting things like anxiety and burnout spiral out of control? These mental skills will determine how far you go, and whether you enjoy yourself on the journey.

Long after your days as a competitive athlete are behind you, the mentality you cultivate will stay with you. We know this because it's been true in our own lives. The work ethic Kim learned playing hockey got her through rigorous academics at Harvard, years of graduate school, defending her dissertation with a week-old baby, and eventually writing this book while raising four teenagers. The self-compassion Jonathan learned by recovering from sports injuries—including torn menisci and concussions—now shapes how he works with athletes, from college players to members of the NFL and MLB.

Although you may be used to thinking of your body as your superpower, we hope this book has convinced you that your mind is the real secret weapon. While your body might be your most obvious asset, your mind is the most versatile one—and it's your mentality that determines whether you simply accumulate wins or truly flourish.

We hope the tools we've presented here bring you the success you dream of—and the mindset you need to truly enjoy it. Amidst all the sweat, hard work, and sacrifice that go along with playing sports, we hope you always stay connected to the kernel of bliss that brought you here in the first place—and always remember your worth as both an athlete *and* a human being.

about the authors

www.mentalitywins.com

Dr. Jonathan Haywood Jenkins, Psy.D, CMPC, is the founder of Mental Fitness & Psychotherapy, LLC, and has spent over a decade at Massachusetts General Brigham Hospital supporting athletes' mental health and performance. A member of the Harvard Medical School teaching community, he serves as team clinical and performance psychologist for the New England Patriots, behavioral sport psychologist for the Boston Red Sox, and sport psychology consultant for the Para Rowing Foundation. He is also the author of *Wednesday Afternoons with Dr. J.*, a children's book he wrote to encourage youth to be brave in therapy. Jonathan attended Guilford College (B.S., Psychology) where he played varsity lacrosse, and he later obtained his Doctorate in Clinical Psychology from the University of Denver's Graduate School of Professional Psychology. He enjoys spending time out in nature with his family, preferably after stealing one of his wife's awesome chocolate chip cookies.

Dr. Kimberly H. McManama O'Brien, PhD, LICSW, is the founder and director of Unlimited Resilience, LLC, a therapy and sport psychology practice for athletes by athletes, and the co-founder and director of Athletes Better Together, an athlete peer mentoring program. Kim has co-authored over seventy-five articles and book chapters related to adolescent suicide, substance use, and mental health, and was awarded the Young Investigator Research Award from the American Foundation for Suicide Prevention in 2019. She is also the co-author of *Emotionally Naked: A Teacher's Guide to Preventing Suicide and Recognizing Students at Risk*. Kim received her undergraduate degree from Harvard University, where she was a four-year member and co-captain of the hockey team, winning a National Championship in 1999. She obtained her MSW and PhD from Boston College and completed her postdoctoral studies at Brown University. When Kim isn't spending time with her husband Kevin and their four children, she can most likely be found coaching, watching, or playing hockey, or out on the paddle courts or golf course.

acknowledgments

Jonathan: I dedicate this book to my two loves: my partner, Molly, and our son, Ford. I'm so fortunate that I get to spend my days with these fun-loving criminals, and that I have the best in-laws, Nana and Papa, that a person could ask for. Thanks Momma Bear, Jason, and Popodopolos for fostering my love of learning and for helping me through difficult times. A BIG thank you to Dr. Ginsburg and Dr. Durant, I'm a better clinician and better person for having had the privilege of working with such amazing mentors. Thank you, Doc Sailes, for all of your support and for encouraging me to write this book, I hope I've done you proud. Thank you to Justin Su'a for seeing something in me that I didn't see myself during our early days together at the Red Sox and giving me the encouragement to continue in this field. Thank you, Jim Whalen, for welcoming me into the Patriots and being such a tremendous mental health advocate. Thanks Richie and Daryl for making our time at the Patriots something truly special. And Dr. Price, I miss you terribly. Thank you for giving me a shot at the Patriots and for always being there when I needed you for personal or professional advice.

Kim: Thank you to all of my clinicians at Unlimited Resilience—you are role models for what professional support for athletes should look and feel like. I am particularly grateful to our kind and compassionate practice manager, Anna Nilsson—you are truly the glue that holds our practice together. Thank you to my team at Athletes Better Together, including all of the amazing mentors who have contributed their stories and experiences to this book. I would be remiss not to mention the GOAT of mentors, Tony Spirito. You believed in me in the beginning of my career when no one else did. More importantly, along the way you have shown me how to bounce back from life's greatest adversities. To my family, you are my everything. I am grateful to have such a full life centered around all of you.

Both of us: First and foremost, this book would not be here without our incredible editor Hilary T. Smith. Hilary, thank you for believing in our words and vision and helping us make this book exceed our expectations. We also want to thank our typesetter, Mayfly Design, and book cover designer, John Frits. Your design contributions have truly elevated the final product. And to all of the athletes we have ever worked with, we dedicate this book to you. We are forever grateful for the honor and privilege to work alongside you in your unique journeys in and out of sport.

bibliography

Altucher, James. *Reinvent Yourself*. North Charleston, SC: CreateSpace Independent Publishing Platform, 2017.

Brach, Tara. *Radical Compassion: Learning to Love Yourself and Your World with the Practice of RAIN*. New York: Penguin, 2020.

Bradford, David L., and Carole Robin. *Connect: Building Exceptional Relationships with Family, Friends, and Colleagues*. Currency, 2021.

Branden, Nathaniel. *The Six Pillars of Self-Esteem*. New York: Bantam, 1994.

Brown, Stuart, and Christopher Vaughan. *Play: How It Shapes the Brain, Opens the Imagination, and Invigorates the Soul*. New York: Avery, 2009.

Christensen, Clayton M., James Allworth, and Karen Dillon. *How Will You Measure Your Life?* Harper Business, 2012.

Clear, James. *Atomic Habits: An Easy and Proven Way to Build Good Habits and Break Bad Ones*. New York: Penguin, 2018.

DeLong, Thomas J. "Three Questions for Effective Feedback." *Harvard Business Review* (blog), August 4, 2011. https://hbr.org/2011/08/three-questions-for-effective-feedback.

Duckworth, Angela. *Grit: The Power of Passion and Perseverance.* New York: Scribner/Simon & Schuster, 2016.

Dweck, Carol S. *Mindset: The New Psychology of Success.* New York: Random House, 2006.

Harden, G. *Stay Sane in an Insane World: How to Control the Controllables and Thrive.* Ashland, OR: Blackstone Publishing, 2023.

Hendriksen, Ellen. *How to Be Enough: Self-Acceptance for Self-Critics and Perfectionists.* New York: St. Martin's Essentials, 2025.

Iaccarino, Anthony. "Ground Truth: Geology and the Origin of Type 2 Fun." *Ridj-it* (blog), February 5, 2024. https://www.ridj-it.com/single-post/ground-truth-geology-and-the-origin-of-type-2-fun.

Jackson, Phil, and Hugh Delehanty. *Sacred Hoops: Spiritual Lessons of a Hardwood Warrior.* New York: Hyperion, 1995.

Jackson, Susan A., and Mihaly Csikszentmihalyi. *Flow in Sports: The Keys to Optimal Experiences and Performances.* Champaign, IL: Human Kinetics, 1999.

Kabat-Zinn, Jon. *Wherever You Go, There You Are: Mindfulness Meditation in Everyday Life.* 10th ed. New York: Hyperion, 2005.

Kerr, James. *Legacy: What the All Blacks Can Teach Us about the Business of Life.* London: Hachette UK, 2013.

Kuzma, Cindy, and Carrie Jackson Cheadle. *Rebound: Train Your Mind to Bounce Back Stronger from Sports Injuries.* London: Bloomsbury Sport, 2019.

McKay, Alan, Brendan Cropley, David Shearer, and Sheldon Hanton. "Developing a 'Clarity of Mind': Exploring a Behaviour-Based Approach to Mental Toughness Development in International Youth Football." *Journal of Applied Sport Psychology* 36, no. 4 (2023): 543–567.

Mumford, George. *The Mindful Athlete: Secrets to Pure Performance.* Berkeley, CA: Parallax Press, 2015.

Neff, Kristin. *Self-Compassion: The Proven Power of Being Kind to Yourself.* New York: William Morrow, 2011.

Nideffer, Robert M. "Anxiety, Attention, and Performance in Sports: Theoretical and Practical Considerations," in *Anxiety in Sports: An International Perspective*, ed. Dieter Hackfort and Charles D. Spielberger (Washington, DC: Hemisphere, 1989), 117–136.

Park, Sung-Ho, Byung-Soo Lim, and Sang-Tae Lim. "The Effects of Self-Talk on Shooting Athletes' Motivation." *Journal of Sports Science & Medicine* 19, no. 3 (2020): 517–521.

Rubin, Rick. *The Creative Act: A Way of Being.* New York: Penguin Press, 2023.

Rupprecht, Anton G. O., Ulrich S. Tran, and Peter Gröpel. "The Effectiveness of Pre-Performance Routines in Sports: A Meta-Analysis." *International Review of Sport and Exercise Psychology* 17, no. 1 (2024): 39–64.

Ruiz, Montse C., John S. Raglin, and Yuri L. Hanin. "The Individual Zones of Optimal Functioning (IZOF) Model (1978–2014): Historical Overview of Its Development and Use." *International Journal of Sport and Exercise Psychology* 15, no. 1 (2015): 41–63.

Ryan, Conor. "After months of dominance, the 2022–23 Bruins lost four legacy-defining games to their greatest nemesis—themselves." *Boston.com*, May 1, 2023. https://www.boston.com/sports/boston-bruins/2023/05/01/bruins-panthers-season-ends-turnovers-column/

Siegel, Daniel J., and Tina Payne Bryson. *The Whole-Brain Child: 12 Revolutionary Strategies to Nurture Your Child's Developing Mind*. New York: Delacorte Press, 2011.

Vora, Ellen. *The Anatomy of Anxiety: Understanding and Overcoming the Body's Fear Response*. New York: Harper Wave, 2022.

Yun, Dongting, Liwei Zhang, Yue Qiu, Robert Schinke, and Jiao Liu. "The Usefulness of the Useless: How Ritualized Behavior Improves Self-Control under Competition Pressure." *Journal of Applied Sport Psychology* 36, no. 3 (2024): 484–498.